Religious Studies Bundle

Philosophy of Religion
Religious Thought Year 1
Ethics

Andrew Capone
Daniella Dunsmore
Peter Baron

Published by Active Education

www.peped.org

This edition 2017

ISBN-13: 978-1542741415
ISBN-10: 1542741416

Handouts, powerpoints, extracts, articles, links, reviews, news and revision materials available on www.peped.org

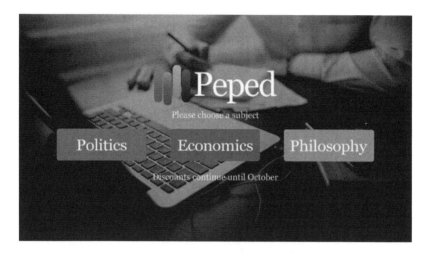

The peped.org website allows students and teachers to explore Philosophy of Religion and Ethics through handouts, film clips, presentations, case studies, extracts, games and academic articles.

Pitched just right, and so much more than a text book, here is a place to engage with critical reflection whatever your level. Marked student essays are also posted.

We also sell digital resources including Teaching Packs for the 2009 and 2016 specifications (full lesson plans, powerpoints, starter activities, and extracts for the entire course), marked essay packs, and a booklet giving full guidelines on how to answer questions on our summer exam paper predictions.

Contents:

Book 1
Philosophy of Religion

OCR Revision Guide

New Spec Year 1

Andrew Capone

Plato

Key Terms

ALLEGORY - A story where the characters and events have a deeper hidden meaning

DOXA - (Greek) Opinion; according to Plato we gain only opinion from experience

EPISTEME - (Greek) Knowledge; according to Plato we gain knowledge through reason, but according to Aristotle we gain knowledge through experience

ETERNAL - That which is timeless and unchanging

FORMS - Or theory of Ideas argues that non-physical (but substantial) forms (or ideas) represent the most accurate reality. When used in this sense, the word form or idea is often capitalised.

TEMPORAL - Of time and changing

The Allegory Of The Cave

Plato presents the allegory of the cave in the Republic to illustrate that experience can only give us **DOXA** and that **EPISTEME** can only come through the knowledge of the **FORMS**.

The Allegory

Prisoners are chained in a cave where they have been since birth and have only ever seen a wall on which **SHADOWS** appear, caused by puppets being carried behind them. When they hear noises they assume that these noises originate from the shadows as this is all they have ever known. When one of the prisoners is freed and takes the journey up the jagged path into the sunlight, at first, he will not understand what he sees as he is used to life in the cave. However, given time, his sight will adjust and he will realise that what he now sees, the puppets, the world etc. is the reality, given life by the sun, and that what he experienced in the cave was the illusion. Further, Plato suggests that if the freed prisoner where to venture back into the cave with tales of what is real outside the cave, his former fellow prisoners would reject what he says and will try to kill him.

The Symbols Of The Allegory

THE CAVE - The physical world of experiences in which we are born, live and die

THE PRISONERS - Normal people who experience the world and take what they experience as reality

THE SHADOWS - Things that we sense in the world through sight, hearing, taste etc.

THE PUPPETS - The **FORMS** which exist in a temporal world of ideas; they are the ideas that we recognise in the things we experience, e.g. love, truth, beauty etc.

THE JAGGED PATH - The journey of the philosopher from ignorance to knowledge

THE SUN - The Essential **FORM** of Goodness which is the highest of all **FORMS** and is responsible for giving life to all things and through which all other **FORMS** can be known

The allegory teaches us that while we think we are gaining knowledge from the **PHYSICAL** world, we are in fact learning nothing but opinion which is constantly changing.

In the same way that the prisoners are chained in the cave and only experience the **SHADOWS** on the wall, we are chained to our reality and only experience the temporal particulars of this physical world. In the same way that the free prisoner gains true knowledge by being freed from his restraints, crawling up the jagged path and seeing how the puppets cast shadows on the wall, we must free ourselves from our reliance on this world, become philosophers and accept that the truth lies in the abstract **FORMS** and that only then can we see the truth.

The Theory Of Forms

Plato's Theory of **FORMS** stipulates that all things that we experience in this world are poor imitations of the true **FORMS** which exist abstractly in the World of Forms. Plato argues that when we experience particulars, for example trees, cats, acts of affection, we are in fact experiencing a fleeting and changing example but in the example we are "recognising" the true **FORM** that is reflected through the example.

As an example, Plato suggested that when we walk through a forest a fool would comment: "Ah, look at all these different trees: elm, oak, ash, there are so many different trees in the forest."

However, the philosopher knows better and so comments, "Look at all these different examples around me, they all appear different but share some similar qualities: they have trunks, branches and leaves. They all possess tree-ness and are all poor imitations of the perfect **FORM** of tree."

The **FORMS** are ideas that we can recognise in all things we experience, for example: tree-ness, table-ness, man-ness, love-ness, red-ness etc. Everything we encounter there are inherent ideas that we can recognise and which we can recognise in other things also.

This lends to the theory the proposition that the ideas are **ABSTRACT** and that the particulars are only temporal and so do not contain any knowledge within them.

The Essential **FORM** of the Good was the way Plato was able to respond to **RELATIVISM**. It is through the **FORM** of the good that anything can be known and it is by this **FORM** that we can behave in a good manner. For Plato, things were only good if they were clear reflections of their **FORMS** and this was only possible if an example was filled with goodness. Essentially, the **FORM** of the good is like a light – hence the sun association in the allegory – which shines through the **FORM**.

The clearer the light shines through, the closer the example is to the **FORM** and the better it is.

For example, the idea of chair-ness is reflected into an example of a new and comfortable chair. Goodness is shining clearly through the new chair such that the example is a close reflection of the **FORM** of chair. However, over time and misuse the chair becomes squeaky, torn and broken such that no longer is much **GOODNESS** shining through the **FORM** so the example is old and broken and no longer a clear reflection of the **FORM** of chair. However, the **FORM** of chair never changes; it is eternal as are all the **FORMS** e.g. maths, love, justice. They are all eternal and cannot change.

Justice is a **FORM** of knowing right from wrong. For Plato, if goodness shines through you, you are good, like the chair, you are a clear reflection of the **FORM** of man and the Essential **FORM** of Good is being shone through the **FORM** into you.

If you are a tyrant, then you are bad reflection.

Strengths

- **Democritus**: All things in the universe can be constantly divided until we come to non-divisible blocks (atoms). While Scientists thought they found them (atoms) they were wrong as they can also be divided.

- **Plato**: Reason enlightened us to what experience failed to find.

- **Heraclitus**: The world is in constant flux meaning that it was constantly changing. The famous quote: "you can never step in the same river twice" highlights this view. **Plato**: Experience gives only changing opinions; the world is one of shadow, not absolutes.

- **Parmenides**: If you take a snapshot image of an arrow flying you will see that at any given point the arrow is stationary. **Plato**: The eternal World of **FORMs** is fixed and unchanging; all **FORMs** that ever existed did so eternally and nothing came into or went out of existence.

- **Pythagoras**: Pythagoras' theorem suggests that some things are true abstractly and are ideas that exist ethereally and are unchanging. **Plato**: Some things are unchanging and exist eternally, the **FORMs**.

Weaknesses

- **Third Man Argument**: Plato says that the FORM of a man is still a man. Therefore, if all men need a FORM of man, and the FORM of man is also a man, then the men **AND** FORM of man together need a FORM, which we might call the FORM of **MAN+**. But the FORM of **MAN+** is itself a man and so the series continues ad infinitum.

- **Extent of the World of FORMS**: It seems bizarre to think of such **FORMS** existing eternally. If would suggest that there are **FORMS** of every conceivable past present and future concept, even things that have not been invented yet and things that are clear negations of things.

Key Quotes

1. "There is not a third man or horse besides the ideal and the individuals" Aristotle, Metaphysics

2. "There are certain forms, whose names these other things have through getting a share of them – as, for instance, just and beautiful has a share of justice and beauty". Plato

3. "A general idea or concept is unchangeable, timeless, intellectually understandable because it is an independently existing real thing or entity… The immortality of the soul is proved by our ability to apprehend the everlasting concept - objects that Plato often calls the Forms". Gilbert Ryle

4. "All metaphysics including its opponent positivism speaks the language of Plato". Martin Heidegger

5. "The Platonic idealist is the man by nature so wedded to perfection that he sees in everything not the reality, but the faultless ideal which the reality misses and suggests". George Santayana

Confusion To Avoid

Plato's Theory of **FORMS** and the Allegory of the Cave all part of Plato's Theory of Knowledge. If a question asks about the **FORMS**, the Allegory can be used to support and justify what the **FORMS** are. Likewise, if the question is about the Allegory, the question expects some explanation of what it was told to explain, that being the **FORMS** themselves.

Possible Exam Questions

1. Critically compare Plato's Form of the Good with Aristotle's Prime Mover.

2. "In their attempts to make sense of reality, Plato relies too much on rationalism and Aristotle relies too much on empirical observation". Discuss

3. Assess the claim that Plato does not value experience enough.

4. 'Plato's Theory of Forms explains how we know what we know.' Discuss

Aristotle

Key Terms

CAUSE - The reason why something exists

EFFICIENT - The agent or agents that cause something else to exist

GOOD - Not needing improvement

NECESSARY - The belief that the Prime Mover cannot not exist

TELOS - The final end of things, what they are made to do, the reason why they are brought into being

Four Causes

All things have four causes: these are the material, formal, efficient and final causes.

MATERIAL CAUSE - The material cause of what a thing is made of. All things are made of material which could be turned into a variety of different things, like wood, metal or wax. The material cause is the basic materials that make up anything. Many things are made of a combination of materials which together form the object. Regardless, all things are made of material.

FORMAL CAUSE - The formal cause is what a thing is. All things come in a raw state, like a block of wax or iron ore, and are then worked into a particular form. Some objects are formed from many different materials, but all things have a form. Even materials in their raw state are in a form and that form being the raw state of the material. Everything is a form of something, e.g. the form of pencil, the form of candle or the form of computer.

EFFICIENT CAUSE - The efficient cause is the agent that brings a thing about. It is the reason why there is a thing at all. A block of marble stone is actually a block of marble stone with a potential to become a statue. It must be moved from that potential state to the actual state of being a statue by an agent or agents who themselves may be using tools to make this reduction possible. This agent or agents that move the marble block into the statue are the efficient cause.

FINAL CAUSE - The final cause is what a thing is made to do, its purpose or **TELOS**. Everything exists for a reason and that reason is the final cause, the ultimate end for any object within its actual state. Objects in a raw state, e.g. iron ore have no man-made purpose as they are naturally occurring but may well have a natural purpose unknown to us. Living objects like trees and animals have their own purposes to survive and reproduce. Everything has a purpose and we know more when we learn what things are for. For example, the appendix in the human body was believed to have no purpose, however, many debate that it does serve a vital function to house good bacteria.

Prime Mover

Aristotle's theory of four causes can be used to build the case for the Prime Mover.

From Potentiality and Actuality

If all things are made of matter in a particular form, then the world itself is also made of material with a form. Motion is the reduction from **POTENTIALITY** (the raw material) to **ACTUALITY** (what it actually is, its form). Therefore, the world must have been moved from its raw material into the form of the world but some Prime Mover. Further, all things which are moved from one state to another must ultimately be moved by some Prime Mover.

From Cause and Effect

All things have an **EFFICIENT CAUSE**, a cause for them to exist at all, and a purpose for which it exists. It then follows that the world itself needs a cause and has some purpose. There must then be some efficient cause that has caused the world to exist for some purpose.

Characteristics Of The Prime Mover

The Prime Mover must have certain characteristics by definition of its nature as Prime Mover:

Pure Actuality - The Prime Mover cannot itself be moved otherwise it would not be the first mover at all. Therefore, it must be pure actuality incapable of being moved itself.

Simple - Given that it is pure actuality, the Prime Mover cannot be a complex being like humans, as complexity implies complex form and motion.

Good - The Prime Mover cannot change and so cannot be improved.

This being the case, the Prime Mover must be perfect, incapable of improving, and so must be perfectly good.

Strengths

- **EMPIRICAL** - Aristotle's approach has been adopted as the basic **EMPIRICAL** approach to science and the development in understanding the world. By analysing the causes of things we can learn what things are and why they behave the way they do. It is the basis of what is called the **SCIENTIFIC METHOD**.

- **SCIENTIFIC PROGRESS -** The Aristotelian approach is the basis of the scientific method. The scientific method is to experience the world, observe it, make hypothesis of how things work, test them and revise our hypothesis. Sometimes this process revolutionises how we think about ourselves: the sun no longer orbits the earth (Copernican revolution) and the Darwinian revolution suggests humankind evolved, rather than being created by God from 'the dust of the ground' (as in Genesis 1 & 2).

- **EXPERIENTIAL** - Experience is the only tool we have as everything we do in life relies on our experiences, from the first instincts to reach for our mothers to our desires to travel and build space ships.

- **REASONABLE** - If we think rationally about Plato's and Aristotle's theories of knowledge, there is far more that we can relate to in Aristotle's approach. It is more rational as it does not exclude experience.

Weaknesses

- **INCOMPLETE** - Aristotle's theory of knowledge was not complete and his own deductions based on his experiences were not always correct.

- **UNRELIABILITY OF EXPERIENCE** - Aristotle's observations were the first steps in our understanding of many things including medicine and technology, however, he himself made incorrect observations about things that could easily be discerned, for example the number of legs on a fly.

- **SUPERIORITY OF REASON** - The example of Democritus and the atoms exemplifies the problem of experience as a substitute for reason. Reason can consider abstract ideas in a way that experience simply cannot.

- **CAUSATION CAN'T BE INFERRED** - When postulating the existence of the Prime Mover, Aristotle infers its existence from the four causes. However, as William of Ockham and David Hume later argue, you cannot infer a causal connection between two things; you can only describe the apparent connection.

Key Quotes

1. "The substance or form is actuality. It is obvious that actuality is prior in substantial being to potency; and one actuality always precedes another in time right back to the actuality of the eternal prime mover." Aristotle

2. "But the primary essence has not matter; for it is complete reality. So the unmovable first mover is one both in definition and in

number". Aristotle

Confusion To Avoid

Do not confuse Aristotle's **FORMAL CAUSE** with Plato's **FORMS.** Plato's **FORMS** are abstract ideas that give rise to all things that we experience in the world. The **FORM** of tree for Plato is the tree-ness we recognise in the various examples of trees that we encounter in the world. However, for Aristotle, upon encountering various different trees, oak, elm, ash etc. we see the similarities and then label those different examples with a similar form by a term, i.e. tree. Aristotle's method is **A POSTERIORI**, from observation and experience.

Possible Exam Questions

1. 'Aristotle successfully proves the existence of the Prime Mover.' Discuss.

2. Assess Aristotle's argument for the Four Causes.

3. "Aristotle's reliance on empiricism has many weaknesses". Discuss

4. Evaluate whether Plato's rationalism is superior to Aristotle's empiricism in making sense of reality.

Soul, Mind and Body - Dualism

Key Terms

DUALISM - the idea that mind and body are distinct substances

MATERIALISM - the idea that mind and body can be explained by physical or material interactions

FALLACY, CIRCULAR REASONING - When the conclusion is implied in the premises

FALLACY, HOMUNCULUS - (Greek, 'little man') A logical fallacy where a problem is explained by the same problem it seeks to explain

FALLACY, INVALID - A fallacy where the conclusion does not flow from the premises

FALLACY, UNSOUND - A fallacy where one or more of the premises are not true

TRIPARTITE NATURE OF THE SOUL - In Platonic Dualism, the belief that the soul is made of three parts: reason, spirit and appetite

Platonic Dualism

IN PHAEDRUS - Plato presents the analogy of the **CHARIOTEER** to illustrate the tripartite nature of the soul:

- **Reason**: The highest part of the soul linked to the role of the guardian in Plato's perfect society; the rational soul is the part of the soul that thinks, reflects and learns. It is centred in the brain and is represented by the **CHARIOTEER** who must control the two horses to maintain the course of the chariot.

- **Spirit**: The emotive part of the soul linked to the role of the auxiliaries in Plato's perfect society; the emotive soul is the part of the soul that is brave, emotional and fights. It is centred in the breast and is represented by the **WHITE HORSE** that pulls the chariot in the direction of emotive conflict.

- **Appetite**: The lowest part of the soul linked to the role of the workers in Plat's perfect society; the appetite is the part of the soul that desires, craves and motivates. It is centred in the abdomen and is represented by the wild **BLACK HORSE** that pulls the chariot in the direction of self-destructive craving.

If it can be demonstrated that people's behaviour reflects the tripartite soul, then it can be argued that the soul exists as a separate entity to the body and as such that we have a dualistic nature: body and soul separate.

IN REPUBLIC - Plato presented a version of the Myth of Er, a soldier who died in battle but whose body did not decompose. Instead his soul went to the plane where the dead go and he witnessed the souls of his comrades being judged and going to different destinations, some into the sky and some into the ground. Additionally, he witnessed souls emerging from the sky, having been rewarded, and the ground, having been punished, and then choosing new lives before drinking from the river of forgetfulness only to be born again.

This process myth was borrowed from the **REINCARNATION** beliefs of Pythagoras. Plato called it transmigration of the soul, as the soul moved from one body to another. When in the ethereal plane, not only were they punished or rewarded, but they also gained all knowledge of the **FORMS** before forgetting it all again only to be born. This belief explains the Plato's view of how the soul is distinguished from the body and can exist independently of it.

IN PHAEDO - Plato presents his three arguments for life after death:

- **Argument from Opposites**: All things are in constant motion between two extremes, e.g. all different temperatures are a flux between hot and cold; all different lengths are a flux between long and short. All opposites are extremes and Heraclitus' **LOGOS** was what prevented any extreme being surpassed. We can observe these opposites in life and so we can be certain of them. In the same way, then, life must have its opposite in death. In the same way that things move from hot to cold and then to hot again we must accept that we move from life to death and then to life again.

- **Argument from Recollection**: All knowledge comes from the FORMs which are eternal ideas that we cannot experience. When we are in the World of FORMs in between lives we know them intimately, and then we forget about them. When on earth, our experiences are in fact us recollecting the FORMs that we see in the examples we encounter. When I see a tree I recollect tree-ness within it. This would only be possible if I already had possessed the knowledge of tree-ness from some previous existence. For Plato, this recollection is proof that we existed previously to our births from where we recall that knowledge.

- **Argument from Affinity**: Plato identifies two kinds of existence, the physical and the non-physical. He shows how all things that we encounter physically have a non-physical affinity. For each tree, there is the non-physical tree-ness, for the act of affection there is the non-physical idea of affection. Likewise, for each life there is the non-physical self. Cebes challenges this by giving the example of the music played that ends when the instrument is destroyed, but Plato insists that the affinity of a person is an eternal affinity.

In these arguments, Plato is presenting his case for why life after death cannot be refuted but instead must be accepted as a reality. It is based in the nature of dualism and is embedded in the theory of the World of **FORMS**.

Cartesian Dualism

For Descartes the soul is a **SPIRITUAL** entity that resided within the body. The soul exists throughout the body and operates in all parts of it. The part of the body, however, which was most associated with the operation of the soul, is the **PINEAL GLAND** in the base of the brain. From here, the soul moved the body around by way of directing the spirit through the ventricles and arteries and thus operating the body like some super marionette.

Descartes chose the pineal gland as, in his time, it was believed that the pineal gland otherwise had no purpose in the brain, and secondly because, while the rest of the brain was divisible into two halves, everything from the left mirroring everything on the right, the pineal gland appeared indivisible. In this way, Descartes was building an **ANATOMICAL** picture for the operations of the soul's interaction with the body.

One way of better understanding Descartes' view of the soul's interaction with the body is to compare it to the cardiovascular system (this is NOT an example given by Descartes).

System	Cardiovascular system	The soul
Stuff that moves through the system	Blood	Spirit
Areas that stuff operates through	Heart	Pineal Gland
Function of the stuff	Takes energy/oxygen round the body	Move the body

Strengths

- **CHILD DEVELOPMENT** - Of Platonic Dualism - Anthony Kenny supported the idea that the psyche develops in his observation of the tantrums of toddlers. They know they crave and have the emotions to cry but have no intellect to know how to control those feelings.

- **REALISTIC** - In the same way we can support Plato's argument for the **FORMS**, we can support Plato's rational approach to the self and the dualistic psyche. Many would argue that there is a part of us that is separate from the body that makes our character.

- **EASTERN PHILOSOPHY** - Many eastern traditions have adopted reincarnation as part of their belief system. These can be used to support Plato's argument for the World of FORMS. In fact, the work of Dr Ian Stevenson on reincarnation is modern scientific evidence to support the belief in **REINCARNATION**. He recorded thousands of reincarnation accounts which, though not conclusive of anything, stand as evidence to support Plato's claims.

Of Cartesian Dualism - Cartesian Dualism supports Plato's dualism and helps us to see how the body and soul can interact in a measurable way.

Weaknesses

Of Platonic Dualism - Plato's Argument from Opposites is in fact impossible to infer.

- **UNPROVABLE** - Plato's two arguments of recollection and affinity are all part of the argument for the World of **FORMS** which Aristotle challenged. If this theory of knowledge can be attacked it undermines the whole argument for dualism.

- **HERESY** - Dualism is rejected by the Catholic Church and considered heresy at least in the sense that Gnosticism is a heresy (the view that body is evil, the soul good). The Catholic Catechism states that the soul is the **FORM** of the body and they were created, and are, one. "Because man is a composite being, spirit and body, there already exists a certain tension in him; a certain struggle of tendencies between "spirit" and "flesh" develops. But in fact this struggle belongs to the heritage of sin. It is a consequence of sin and at the same time a confirmation of it. It is part of the daily experience of the spiritual battle", Catechism 2516.

- **SCIENTIFICALLY FALSE** - Of Cartesian Dualism - The reality is that much of Descartes' ideas were demonstrated to be false and in fact poor science. The pineal gland is the part of the brain that secretes Melatonin and in no way can it house or direct a soul.

- **CATEGORY ERROR** - Gilbert Ryle accused Descartes of committing a category error in which he categorises the body as one type of stuff and the soul as another. He gives an example of a visitor at Oxford who asks to see the university and is guided around the campus and sees the dorms, the registry office, the fields etc. But then he asks "where is the university?" It is a category error to think that the university is more than the sum of its parts. In the same way Descartes is wrong to think that the person is more than the sum of its body. There is no other self or soul that makes the person.

- **HOMUNCULUS FALLACY** - Descartes also commits the homunculus fallacy in that the argument that the soul directs the body leaves us with a similar problem to explain what drives the soul itself.

Key Quotes

1. "The body is the source of endless trouble to us by reason of the mere requirement of food; and is liable also to disease which overtake and impede us in the search after true being: it fills us full of loves, and lusts, and fears, and fancies of all kinds, and endless foolery and in fact, as men say, takes away all power of thinking". Plato

2. "I shall often speak of it, with deliberate abusiveness, as 'the dogma of the Ghost in the Machine'. I hope to prove that it is entirely false, and false not in detail but in principle. It is not merely an assemblage of particular mistakes. It is one big mistake and a mistake of a special kind. It is, namely, a category-mistake". Gilbert Ryle

3. "Descartes split thought from existence and identified existence with reason itself: (I think therefore I am). How different from the approach of St Thomas, for whom it is not thought which determines existence, but existence "esse" which determines thought! I think the way I think because I am that which I am." John Paul II

Confusion To Avoid

The analogy of the **CHARIOTEER** does not describe how the psyche drives the body. The charioteer is not the psyche and the chariot is not the body. The charioteer and horses are the whole psyche in its tripartite nature (**REASON, SPIRIT, APPETITE**).

Plato's dualism might be improbable/unprovable; it is not inconsistent. Following Plato's reasoning it is acceptable to conclude the existence of the World of **FORMS**. To undermine the whole you need to attack dualism, or the arguments for the Theory of **FORMS**. Similarly, we cannot prove reincarnation. Given the nature of the spiritual realm you would never be able to, so absence of evidence is not evidence of absence.

Possible Exam Questions

1. Assess the claim that disembodied existence is possible.

2. "The body is separate from the soul." Discuss

3. "The concept of the soul is best understood as a metaphor." Discuss

4. "The mind/body distinction is a category error." Evaluate this view.

Soul, Mind and Body - Monism

Key Terms

ANIMA - In Aristotle's De Anima, the anima is the soul of a person

HYLOMORPHIC SOUL/BODY UNITY - Aristotle's interpretation of monism, that the body and soul are a unity and cannot be separated from each other (Greek, **HYLE** = form, **MORPHE** = matter)

IDENTITY THEORY - The theory that all mental activities including emotion and intelligence are centred in the brain

MONISM - The belief that the body and soul are one and the same and that the soul cannot exist independently of the body

SELF-IDENTITY - The person you are besides your physical body

Aristotelian Monism

Aristotle presented his ideas concerning the soul in his work **DE ANIMA**. In the work, Aristotle discusses the nature of the relationship between the body and the soul all stemming from his earlier argument for the **FOUR CAUSES**. Aristotle argues that the body and soul make up a **HYLOMORPHIC** body/soul unity. For Aristotle, there is no separate soul, but rather, the soul is the **FORM** and purpose of the body, the body in action. This can be seen through his explanation of potentiality and actuality and then of cause and effect.

The human being is matter in some form fulfilling some **TELOS**. Then the soul is the **ACTUALITY** of the body. Aristotle gives the wax stamp example to emphasise the unity between the body and soul. The stamp cannot be removed from the wax as they are one unity. Likewise, whatever it is that makes the soul, the appearance, shape, character, personality etc. it is all part of the physical person; the soul is the form of the body, the actuality of the flesh.

- **First potentiality** – our material self.

- **Second potentiality/first actuality** – our formal self.

- **Second actuality** – our purpose being engaged.

The soul is animation: the person engaging with their purpose which is determined by their form and doing what they are supposed to be doing. As Aristotle said, if an axe had a soul it would be chopping; if an eye had a soul it would be seeing. We have a soul, and that is to engage with **REASON** and live the good life.

Therefore, there can be no question of the soul existing disembodied as the soul is the **ANIMATION** of the body. It is not a separate thing that can exist separately. The body and soul are a **HYLOMORPHIC** soul/body unity.

Identity Theory - Identify Theory is a belief that a person's self-identity is linked directly to their physical body. It is a materialist approach formed from a series of scholarly ideas and beliefs:

- **BODY OR MIND?** John Locke - John Locke was the 17th Century philosopher who presented the thought experiment of a prince and cobbler who wake up in each other's bodies. When he wakes up, the prince presents himself to the palace but is sent out as he appears as the cobbler. The thought experiment asks us to consider what the person is: the physical person or the mind inside. It asks us to consider whether or not a person could even theoretically switch bodies or whether we identify the person's self with their physical person.

- **BODY OR PERSONALITY?** Phineas Gage - Phineas Gage was a 19th Century railroad construction foreman who suffered the fate of having a metal pole through his brain. While he survived, he was forever changed as a person, from being approachable and friendly, to being short tempered and easily angered. This suggests that the character of a person, or their soul, is directly linked to the physical brain itself, not some spiritual substance.

- **BODY OR GENES?** Richard Dawkins - Richard Dawkins argues that the body is a survival machine for the genes which survive within us. They last forever if they are successful and they determine everything about our character and person. We should therefore not consider ourselves special in any particular way as we are governed by our genes and the idea of a life after death is simply a **MEME** that our brains have created in order to cope with the reality of our fate.

Strengths

- **TRUE TO SCIENCE** - Of Aristotle's Monism - Aristotle's interpretation of the soul as the **ANIMATION** of the body fits well with all modern scientific attitudes as the soul can be seen in light of the brain's activity and personal identity. It does not force the believer to accept an abstract world or a spiritual dimension.

- **TRUE TO THE BIBLE** - John Hick supports Aristotle's **MONISM** when he argues that the only self we can know is the empirical self. He argues that God has made us as a psycho-somatic soul/body unity, and that the resurrection of Christ was a purely bodily resurrection. This is supported by the letters of St Paul when he describes resurrection as being with a 'spiritual body'.

- **TRUE TO PSYCHOLOGY** - Of Identity Theory - Identity Theory can be demonstrated by observing how people's behaviour is affected by psychology and a physiology. When we observe people's characters changing on account of drugs and alcohol we are witnessing a change to the character which supports the idea that the soul is in fact the character formed by the physical brain.

Weaknesses

- **UNPROVABLE** - Of Aristotle's **MONISM** - Aristotle's Monism is itself difficult to demonstrate beyond doubt. Aristotle did not give a clear indication if there was life after death. He seemed to have allowed for the possibility for the Prime Mover to maintain a person's intelligence but this was never developed.

- **DOESN'T EXPLAIN MOTIVATION** - Of Identity Theory - Stephen Davis argued that Identity Theory only explains the workings of the brain, and not the motivation of the brain. He discusses the brain may be neutral and that the soul is what guides it.

- **THE BRAIN AND MIND REMAIN MYSTERIES** - The reality is that know little about the brain and how it actually works, so everything we claim about how the brain works and how interacts with the body and forms the character is pure speculation.

Key Quotes

1. "Which person was which? Is it the mind that makes the individual, or the body? What makes us what we are? Is it our appearance, our memories, our individual personality traits, or is it something else?" John Locke

2. "Compared the human to a river, once the water is gone from the bed what is left of the river?" Bertrand Russell

3. "After some disaster when the 'Dead' and the 'Survivors' have both been listed, what logical space is left for a third category, 'Both'?" Anthony Flew

4. "God didn't promise Abraham eternal life as an individual. But he did promise him something else. Abraham was in no doubt that the future lay with his seed, not his individuality. God knew Darwinism." Richard Dawkins

5. "Consciousness, for the purpose of this story, can be thought of as the culmination of an evolutionary trend towards the emancipation of survival machines as executive decision-takers from their ultimate masters, the genes." Richard Dawkins

Confusion To Avoid

Aristotle was not a **MATERIALIST**, he was a **MONIST.**

Materialist approaches, including Identity Theory, are suppositions and speculations, not proofs. It would be wrong to assume that it has proven anything concrete about the nature of the body and soul. In fact, there is arguably more evidence for **REINCARNATION** than Identity Theory, both from the number of believers to the work of Dr Ian Stevenson (see Strengths of Dualism).

Possible Exam Questions

1. "The body and soul cannot be separated." Discuss.

2. Assess whether the soul is best considered as reality or as metaphor.

3. Evaluate what Aristotle meant by arguing that the soul is the form of the body.

4. "The body dies, but the soul lives forever". Discuss

The Ontological Argument

Key Terms

A PRIORI - Before experience

A POSTERIORI - After experience

ANALYTIC - Self-evident knowledge, known a priori

CONTINGENT - Something that does not need to exist but depends on something else to exist

DE DICTO - By word/definition

DE RE - In reality/the real world

NECESSARY - Something that cannot not be the case

PREDICATE - The predicate is the part of a sentence (or clause) which tells us what the subject does or is eg God (subject) exists (predicate)

SYNTHETIC - Matters of fact, descriptions of how things are, known a posteriori

Anselm's First & Second Version

Proslogion Chapter 1: Dealing with the Fool

Anselm reflected on Psalm 14: 'The fool has said in his heart "there is no God"'. For Anselm, it was a matter of foolishness for anyone to know what God is and maintain that there is no God. He therefore set out to demonstrate that God's existence can be proven **ANALYTICALLY,** as a matter of reason, from what we mean by God. He sought to prove that God existed necessarily and that this could be shown **A PRIORI.**

Proslogion Chapter 2: Ontological Argument Version 1

Premise 1: God is a being than which nothing greater can be conceived.

By definition, when any person discusses God, they know what they mean by the term. They mean the God of **CLASSICAL THEISM.** This God is not a powerful being that can be beaten in power by some other being, but rather is the most powerful being possible even in imagination. If you can imagine a being greater than God, then what you were originally thinking about was not God. God is a being such that no greater being can possibly be imagined.

Premise 2: It is greater to exist in the mind and reality than the mind alone.

Anselm is implying that existence is a **PREDICATE** of God's nature. Anselm uses the example to demonstrate this point. When a painter conceives of a painting, he has that idea in his mind but it is not yet in reality. When he paints it, he has it on the canvas and when he contemplates it now, the idea of the existing painting, compared to the idea of the paining before it was painted, is greater. Therefore, it is greater to exist in the mind and reality than only in the mind. Put bluntly, a £10 note is better than the idea of a £10 note.

Conclusion: God must exist.

If it is the case that God is a being than which nothing greater can be conceived and existing in the mind and reality is greater than the mind alone, then if God only existed in the mind, he would not be the greatest possible being, as theoretically, a God that did exist would be greater than a God that did not exist. Of the two: God that exists in the mind and reality and God that exists in the mind alone, the God that exists in the mind and reality is the greater. And since God is that than which nothing greater can be conceived, God must be the God that exists in the mind and reality. So God must exist in reality, so God must exist.

Proslogion Chapter 3: Ontological Argument Version 2

Premise 1: God is a being than which nothing greater can be conceived.

Premise 2: Necessary existence is greater than **CONTINGENT** existence.

If we consider the relationship between necessary and contingent things, we find that **NECESSARY** things are greater as they cannot not exist, whereas contingent things depend on others and can conceivably not exist. Therefore, necessary existence is greater than contingent existence.

Conclusion: God must necessarily exist.

If God is that than which nothing greater can be conceived, and necessary existence is greater than contingent existence, then surely God must be necessary, as between a necessary God and a contingent one, the necessary God meets the criteria of being that than which nothing greater can be conceived. So God must exist.

Gaunilo's Response

In Behalf Of The Fool, Gaunilo responded to both premises of the first version of Anselm's argument, and so sought to undermine its logic.

Premise 1: God is a being than which nothing greater can be conceived.

Gaunilo argued that it was possible for a person to understand the definition Anselm gave without committing oneself to accepting its existence or even reality. He gave the example of the rumour of a man. If I describe a man in full detail, I would use my understanding of 'men' in general to form the image in my mind. But if I were then told that this man did not exist, it would not affect my understanding of the description. In the same way, I can understand what Anselm means by 'a being than which nothing greater can be conceived' without committing myself to believing it is a real thing.

Premise 2: It is greater to exist in the mind and reality than the mind alone.

Gaunilo challenged the use of existence as a predicate. He argued that one could not simply define God into existence by saying that God's perfection required God to exist. He gave the example of the **PERFECT**

ISLAND. If I were to describe an island that were perfect in every way, I could well imagine it. But to be told that now by virtue of the fact that I understood it to be perfect, I now must accept it exists in reality, is absurd. Gaunilo was arguing that that existence **DE DICTO** (by definition) could not lead to existence **DE RE** (in reality). Ultimately, existence is not a predicate and so we cannot list it among God's attributes.

Apologetic

Anselm replied to Gaunilo by pointing out that it was impossible to compare God to an island as the island is a contingent thing and God is a **NECESSARY** one. Ultimately, the argument's premises only work for God and for no other thing.

Strengths

• **DESCARTES** argued in Meditations that existence was a predicate of God in the same way that three sides is a predicate of triangles. Descartes argued that God's nature was perfection and that existence was an attribute of perfection. God's existence needed to be discovered rather than proven.

• **ALVIN PLANTINGA** in God, Freedom and Evil supported Anselm in his response to Gaunilo's challenge. Plantinga pointed out that the use of the island could not possibly undermine the argument as there was no intrinsic maxim that could make an island perfect, since it was a **CONTINGENT** thing. God on the other hand was a necessary being (in theory) and so it is perfectly reasonable to imaging a perfect God. A perfect island is illogical, a perfect God is not.

- **CHARLES HARTSHORNE** argued in Anselm's Discovery that it was true that existence certainly adds something to the properties of a thing. Discussing the symptoms of a sickness could never compare to actually having it. The existence of the sickness adds to the understanding of it and so we can view the existence of God as something more than just the **DE DICTO** definition.

The first part of Anselm's argument was to show that the man who says there is no God is a fool. This still applies even if we do not follow Anselm so far as to prove that God must exist necessarily **A PRIORI**. Even the atheist must accept the definition of God, **DE DICTO**, as being the creator of all things. This is a given and does not need to be experienced to be understood. This is what we mean by God.

If this is the case, then it is reasonable to postulate that God is not a subject of the universe. God is not within the universe to be discovered or unmasked. God is not Zeus on Mt Olympus or Thor casing lightning bolts.

As creator God would be **TRANSCENDENTALLY OUTSIDE** the universe. This being the case, for any person to state with any kind of certainty that there is no God, is presuming that they can know that there is no transcendent God. Yet there is no way we, as temporal beings, can have any knowledge of what is in existence at the far reaches of the temporal universe, let alone outside of the universe.

Therefore, if a man says in his heart "there is no God" and believes it with all sincerity, then he is a fool. All he can ever say is "I cannot know if there is a God".

Weaknesses

- **AQUINAS** argued in Summa Theologica that God is not self-evident to us and as such we can never know God's nature. The Ontological Argument assumes that we can know God's nature ourselves. This is impossible.

- **IMMANUEL KANT** argued in Transcendental Dialectic that existence could not be a predicate. The statement 'God exists' is of the logical form S is P, that is Subject is Predicate, e.g. Grass is Green. Upon stating that grass is green, we must locate some grass in order to investigate whether or not it is in fact green. Upon finding some we can observe it **A POSTERIORI** and answer either 'yes' or 'no'. To discover if grass exists we must do the same, find some and then investigate. But upon finding the grass we need look no further at it, as we have shown it exists already. Therefore, existence does not operate like other properties that we need to investigate within a subject. (such as shape or colour). So existence is not a predicate of a subject.

- **BERTRAND RUSSELL** argued in Philosophy of Language that when we talk of the existence of things we talk about X, such that X has some predicates. We search for an X to match these predicates and then state 'yes, there is an example' or 'no, there is not'. This is a process of **INSTANTIATION** (providing a specific, real world example of an abstract idea). When we discuss existence we are seeking to instantiate it. We cannot say a thing exists if we cannot instantiate it a posteriori. If we cannot instantiate God, then we can never say "God exists".

Key Quotes

1. 'The fool says in his heart "there is no God".' Psalm 14:1-3

2. "There is doubt that there exists a being, than which nothing greater can be conceived, and it exists both in the understanding and in reality." Anselm

3. "If a man should try to prove to me by such reasoning that this island truly exists, and that its existence should no longer be doubted, either I should believe that he was jesting, or I know not which I ought to regard as the greater fool." Gaunilo, In Behalf of the Fool

4. "Because we do not know the essence of God, the proposition [God exists] is not self-evidence to us; but needs to be demonstrated by things that are more known to us." Aquinas, Summa Theologica

5. "All existential propositions are synthetic." Kant, Transcendental Dialectic

6. "To say something exists is to say it is instantiated, or that it actually does appear in existence, not that it is existence is a predicate." Bertrand Russell, The Philosophy of Language

7. "No matter how great the island is, no matter how many Nubian maidens and dancing girls adorn it, there could always be a greater." Alvin Plantinga, God, Freedom and Evil

Confusion To Avoid

In an essay candidates must always deal with all of Anselm's premises correctly within their respective versions. The challenges of the argument come as challenges to the **PREMISES**. The first that God is in fact a being than which nothing greater can be conceived and that we accept that definition, and the second, that existence is a **PREDICATE**, as existing in reality is better than in the mind alone. To defeat the argument, scholars attack these premises.

Possible Exam Questions

1. 'Anselm's Ontological Argument proves God exists logically.' Discuss.

2. Assess the claim that existence is a predicate.

3. "A priori arguments for God's existence are more persuasive than a posteriori arguments". Discuss

4. Critically evaluate the view that the ontological argument contains a number of logical fallacies which nullify the conclusion that God exists.

The Cosmological Argument

Key Terms

A POSTERIORI - After experience

ACTUALITY - When something is in the state of doing something, e.g. fire is actually hot

CONTINGENT - True by virtue of the way things in fact are, and not by logical necessity

POTENTIALITY - When something has the power to be in another state, e.g. wood has the potential to be hot.

INFINITE REGRESSION - The belief that all things are moved/causes by previous motions/causes going back in time infinitely.

SUFFICIENT REASON - The principle that all things need a total explanation to account for them.

Aquinas' First, Second And Third Way

St Thomas Aquinas presented his first three ways to prove God's existence a posteriori in the Summa Theologica. These form the **COSMOLOGICAL ARGUMENT**.

First Way, From Motion

• Everything is in a state of **MOTION**. This can be observed in the world, e.g. seasons change, plates move in orbits etc.

• Motion is the reduction from **POTENTIALITY** to **ACTUALITY**. E.g. the wood is actually cold but has the potential of being actually hot.

• Nothing can move itself. The wood cannot make itself hot; it must be **MOVED** into a state of heat by a source of heat, e.g. fire.

• Motion cannot regress **INFINITELY**. If there was no first motion, there would be no subsequent motion and therefore no current motion. But we observe motion.

• There must be a **FIRST MOTION** that is itself unmoved. If the first motion were itself moved, then it would not be the first motion. Therefore, the first motion cannot itself be moved. It must be pure **ACTUALITY** and so unmoved.

• This is what we call God. Aquinas is arguing that there is a **FIRST MOVER**. He is then stating the God of Christian faith is in fact this First Mover.

Second Way, From Causality

• Everything is an **EFFECT** that is caused. We can observe cause and effect in our daily life, e.g. parents cause children to exist etc.

• Nothing can cause itself. Everything must be caused by something that is not itself. Rather, things must be caused by something previous to itself.

• Causation cannot regress **INFINITELY**. If there was no first cause, there would be no subsequent effects and therefore no current effects. But we observe cause and effect now.

• There must be a **FIRST CAUSE** that is itself uncaused. If the first cause were itself caused, then it would not be the first cause. Therefore, the first cause cannot be caused. It must be pure cause and so uncaused.

• This is what we call **GOD**. Aquinas is arguing that there is a First Cause. He is then stating the God of Christian faith is in fact this First Cause.

Third Way, From Necessity and Contingency

• All things are **CONTINGENT** (exist because of the way the world happens to be). Everything we observe could potentially not exist; nothing necessarily exists in and of itself.

• All things that exist contingently at one point did not exist. Allowing for an infinite amount of time, there could happily be a time when there was nothing in existence at all.

• Nothing comes from nothing. If ever there was nothing, then, since nothing can come from nothing, there would be nothing at all. But evidently there is something.

• There must be a **NECESSARY EXISTENCE**. In order to account for why there is something at all, we must accept that there is something that cannot not exist, but is necessary.

• This what we call God. Aquinas is arguing that there is a **NECESSARY BEING**. He is then stating the God of Christian faith is in fact this Necessary Being.

Hume's Challenges

David Hume challenged the cosmological argument in Dialogues Concerning Natural Religion and various other writings. The following are three of the most direct challenges.

1. We have no experience of universes being created.

Hume argued that all we can ever know of motion and cause and effect only comes from experience. Since we have never experienced the creation of universes, we can never discuss it with any kind of knowledge or certainty. This can be used to challenge the postulation that all things need movement or initial cause. Since **INFINITE REGRESSION** is a theoretical possibility, and since we have never experienced the supposed 'initial motion/cause', we can never assume there is one.

2. Causation cannot be observed.

Hume took this challenge from **WILLIAM OF OCKHAM** who presented this very challenge against Aquinas himself. The principle of causation itself cannot be experienced and so is assumed. Hume gives the example of the billiard balls. When we see one ball supposedly hitting the other, we are in fact making an **ASSUMPTION**. We never actually experience the connection and causation between them. We just assume it is happening. For all we know the two never touch, and in fact at an atomic level the do not! Additionally, when a man hails a bus, though it appears that he is stopping it, he in fact is not. In this way we can challenge Aquinas as causation is implied, never observed, and so the second way is undermined.

3. 'Necessary being' has no logical meaning.

This challenge was later picked up by **BERTRAND RUSSELL** as a challenge to the logic of the cosmological argument. When Aquinas discusses the idea of a necessary being that is required if there are contingent things, Hume challenges this as the term 'necessary being' has no meaning in itself. Russell supports this by arguing that the only necessary things are **ANALYTIC** propositions, like 'triangles have three sides'. Hume supports Kant's claim that all existential propositions are **SYNTHETIC** and so no being can ever be said to necessarily exist.

Strengths

Aquinas' Cosmological Argument reflects Aristotle's four causes and his argument for the Prime Mover.

• All things are moved from their material cause (potentiality) to their formal cause (actuality). And so if you trace back all movement you must come to a Prime Mover (First Mover).

• All things have an efficient cause (cause) in order to achieve some final cause (effect). And so if you trace back all causes you must come to a Prime Mover (First Cause).

Fr Friedrich Copleston supported the cosmological argument by presenting his version of the argument from contingency in a radio debate with Bertrand Russell in 1948.

• Some things in the world are not the explanation for their own existence, e.g. we depend on our parents to exist and the air we breathe to continue existing.

- The world is the real or imagined aggregate of contingent things. There is no world separate from the aggregate of things in the world. And so nothing about the world explains the existence of it.

- We must look for a total explanation for all things. If we find it all well and good, if not we proceed further until we find a total explanation. This links to Gottfried Leibniz' argument for sufficient reason.

Weaknesses

- **IMMANUEL KANT** argued in Transcendental Dialectic that the process of cause and effect are subjects of the universe and as such we can never infer that they work beyond this universe. For this reason, we can never postulate what 'causes' this universe as we can never look beyond it.

- **BERTRAND RUSSELL** argued in his radio debate with Copleston that the terms used in the cosmological argument hold no meaning. Not only does necessary being mean nothing, and in fact reminded him of the ontological argument, but further, it makes no sense to discuss a total cause. It is enough to know that the striking of the match caused the flame without looking for a total explanation. For this reason, the cosmological argument goes too far in its assumption of what we can know from principles of cause and effect.

- Other problems with the cosmological argument include the problem of **DEISM**. The argument need not conclude that there is a theistic sustaining God, but rather a distant creator. Though Aquinas was cure to state that what we believed God to be was the First Mover. Still this is not proof, just faith.

One modern challenge responds to Aquinas' rejection of infinite regression. Modern physicists do not reject the possibility of infinite regression and many discuss inflation rather than a big bang. It has not escaped them that Einstein's principle that energy cannot be created or destroyed. So how can you have something from nothing?

Key Quotes

1. "The first and more manifest way is the argument from motion. It is certain, and evident to our senses, that in the world some things are in motion." Aquinas, Summa Theologica

2. "Suppose the book of the elements of geometry to have been eternal, one copy always having been written down from an earlier one. It is evident that even though a reason can be given for the present book out of a past one, we should never come to a full reason." Gottfried Leibniz, Theodicy

3. "Nothing is demonstrable, unless the contrary is a contradiction." David Hume, Dialogues Concerning Natural Religion

4. "We find…the transcendental principle whereby from the contingent we infer a cause. This principle is applicable only in the sensible world; outside that world it has no meaning whatsoever." Immanuel Kant, Transcendental Dialectic

5. "This being is either itself the reason for its own existence, or it is not. If it is, well and good. If not, then we must proceed further. But if we proceed to infinity in that sense, then there's no explanation of existence at all." Fr Friedrich Copleston, Radio debate with Bertrand Russell, 1948

6. "The word "necessary" I should maintain, can only be applied

significantly to propositions. And, in fact, only to such as are analytic - that is to say - such as it is self-contradictory to deny." Bertrand Russell, Radio debate with Fr Friedrich Copleston, 1948

Confusion To Avoid

Aquinas was not discussing motion and causation back in time. He was not saying that the first motion or **FIRST CAUSE** were at the start of the universe. The understanding of fixed point creation and the expansion of time and space was not firmly argued scientifically until the 20th Century. Aquinas was referring to first motion and first cause within the universe now. He was describing the nature of a God that sustains the world now, not one that started the world 14 billion years ago.

Possible Exam Questions

1. Assess the claim that the cosmological argument proves that God exists a posteriori.

2. 'Hume's challenges successfully disprove the cosmological argument.' Discuss.

3. "The cosmological argument jumps to the conclusion that there is a transcendental creator without sufficient explanation". Discuss

4. "Aquinas' first three ways provide compelling reasons to believe in God". Discuss

The Teleological Argument

Key Terms

TELOS - (Greek) purpose

ANALOGY - A comparison between two things using one to infer conclusions of the other

FALLACY, BEGGING THE QUESTION - When the conclusion is assumed in the premises

QUA PURPOSE - From purpose, a teleological argument that infers that all things are designed with a purpose

QUA REGULARITY - From regularity, a teleological argument that infers that there is regularity in the universe

Aquinas & Paley

St Thomas Aquinas presented his fifth way to prove God's existence **A POSTERIORI** in the Summa Theologica. This forms his teleological argument.

Fifth Way, From the Governance of the World

• Things that lack intelligence act for an **END**. Things such as natural bodies all act towards some end, e.g. planets orbit stars, plants grow towards the sun and seasons change etc.

- All things act as if **DESIGNED**. Everything works towards its end as though it were designed this way.

- Things that lack knowledge are directed by things with **INTELLIGENCE**. Aquinas gives the example of the archer. The arrow cannot direct itself and so is directed to its mark by the archer.

- Some intelligent being exists to direct all things to their goals. Since everything in the universe moves towards its **PURPOSE** and cannot direct itself, there must be an intelligence that directs these things by governing the universe and moving all things towards their prescribed goals.

- This is what we call God. Aquinas is arguing that there is a **SUPREME INTELLIGENCE**. He is then stating the God of Christian faith is in fact this supreme intelligence.

Paley

William Paley presented his version of the Teleological Argument in his book **NATURAL THEOLOGY**. This was written after David Hume presented his challenges to the teleological argument and so was likely unaware of them. Paley was a biologist of his time and so his arguments are based On observation of nature.

- All things are **FIT FOR PURPOSE**. All natural bodies are suitably designed for their purposes, e.g. pigs' teats are sufficient for feeding a litter; swans' necks are long enough to reach the bottom of ponds; and the eye is perfectly fit for seeing.

• Design needs a **DESIGNER**. If something is perfectly designed to fulfil a purpose, it suggests that there is a designer who designed it for that purpose.

• The **ANALOGY** of the watch suggests that if the watch is designed by a watchmaker, then the world which is infinitely more complex than the watch must itself be designed by a world maker.

Hume's Challenges

David Hume presented his challenges against **TELEOLOGICAL ARGUMENTS** in general, not against any one particular argument. There are many challenges but these are the most succinct:

Fallacy of Analogy

Analogy can only be used when comparing two similar things. When the world is compared to a **MACHINE** and it is inferred that the world must have a maker as the machine has a maker, this is a false use of analogy. He famously said that the world is more like a cabbage than a machine; not because the world is anything like a cabbage, but because it is evidently nothing like a machine.

Fallacy of Inference

Hume argued that just because there appeared to be **ORDER** in the world this does not mean that there is in fact order. This is to infer order where there is no proof of it. In fact, Hume argued, apparent order can come from actual chaos. Since 'order' is self-perpetuating, if all things started in chaos, then when order randomly appears then it maintains itself and we infer an order to it. Just because A then B, does not mean B then A.

Assumption of One God

Hume argued that even if the teleological argument worked in proving that there was a designer God, there is no way that you can assume that there is one God. Hume used the example of the ship being built by many shipwrights to show that it is very possible that there may be **MANY GODS** who are responsible for the world for all we know.

Strengths

- **COMPLEXITY -** The teleological argument includes any observation of nature that leaves us no explanation for its existence other than God. Anthony Flew, following a lifetime of atheism, was finally converted to theism following the reflection of the double helix within DNA. He could no longer deny that the incredible complexity of DNA had no explanation other than God.

- **BEAUTY** - Paul Davies argued in The Mind of God that science has allowed us to better understand the world, and in so doing has allowed us to see how we are connected to an intricate universe. This beauty denotes pattern and intention.

- **CRITIQUE OF DARWINISM** - Michael Behe in Darwin's Black Box argued that there are some things in the universe that are so complex that they cannot be reduced into a simpler predecessor. He gives various examples of this **IRREDUCIBLE COMPLEXITY**, including the flagellum which he argues could not have evolved randomly. Evolution is a theory that organisms have changed over millennia from simpler organisms. Darwin said this worked by the principle of Natural

Selection; however, this only works when you have a variety of variations that can be narrowed down, so the one that is the fittest survives. But what creates the variance is debatable. Richard Dawkins and other atheist biologists argue it is random mutation within species that give this variation. However, Behe's examples challenge this. If there is no way that the flagellum could have randomly appeared then it could not have been naturally selected. (Flagellum = a slender thread-like structure, especially a microscopic whip-like appendage which enables many protozoa, bacteria, spermatozoa, etc. to swim).

Weaknesses

- **MALEVOLENCE** - John Stuart Mill argued in On Nature that if there was a designer of the world, then this designer is either malevolent or stupid to create a world with such natural evil within it. Jean Paul Sartre argued similarly when he discussed this imperfect world. If there is natural evil in a designed world, then it is accountable to the designer.

- **BEGS THE QUESTION** - Richard Swinburne argued in The Essence of God that Aquinas' argument committed the fallacy of begging the question. This is a factor in all teleological arguments where the premises infer design. If a designer is inferred in the premises then the conclusion – the world has a designer – is assumed before it is proven.

- **SCIENTIFICALLY WRONG** - Richard Dawkins argued in The Blind Watchmaker argued that, while Paley was working with the best knowledge of his time, he was utterly wrong as the appearance of the eye, the pigs' teats and the swan's neck can all be accounted for by evolution, not a designer.

Key Quotes

1. "Now whatever lacks intelligence cannot move towards an end, unless it be directed by some being endowed with knowledge and intelligence; as the arrow is shot to its mark by the archer". Aquinas, Summa Theologica

2. "This mechanism being observed, the inference we think is inevitable, that the watch must have had a maker". William Paley, Natural Theology

3. 'We have no data to establish any system of cosmogony. Our experience, so imperfect in itself and so limited both in extent and duration, can afford us no probable conjecture concerning the whole of things.' David Hume, Dialogues Concerning Natural Religion

4. "Aquinas' statement that all things are directed by some mind towards a purpose, and that mind is God, commits the fallacy of begging the question. Things need a purpose, God gives things a purpose, therefore God must be the purpose". Richard Swinburne, The Essence of God

5. "Paley's argument is made with passionate sincerity and is informed by the best biological scholarship of the day, but it is wrong, gloriously and utterly wrong". Richard Dawkins, The Blind Watchmaker

Confusion To Avoid

David Hume wrote twenty-three years before William Paley, so his Dialogues Concerning Natural Religion are not a response to Paley's version of the teleological argument. Though it is tempting to see Hume's challenge as saying that the world is not like a watch, and that the world is more like a cabbage than a watch, this is utterly mistaken. Hume was more likely responding to the **NEWTONIAN MODEL** of the universe which saw it like a machine. Hume was challenging this mechanistic view, as one of his challenges to the cosmological argument was that we cannot experience **CAUSATION** and so we cannot infer this mechanical interpretation of the world.

Possible Exam Questions

1. 'The teleological argument proves that the universe is designed.' Discuss.

2. Assess Hume's challenges of the teleological argument.

3. Critically evaluate a priori against a posteriori arguments for God's existence.

4. Can teleological arguments be successfully defended against the challenge of 'chance' and natural selection?

Religious Experience

Key Terms

NUMINOUS - The apprehension of the wholly other (a sense of wonder)

RELIGIOUS EXPERIENCE, DIRECT - An encounter with God or an experience received from God (voice, vision, miracle etc)

RELIGIOUS EXPERIENCE , INDIRECT - An understanding about God occurring through some temporal experience (birth, sunset, etc)

PSYCHOLOGICAL NEUROSIS - An experience or way of thinking that is explicitly the product of the mind's functions

The Case For Religious Experiences

Religious experiences occur throughout history and can be particularly identified within biblical and Catholic history. These experiences have been explored and investigated to discover what makes an experience religious and what, if anything, can qualify it as genuine.

Characteristics of Religious Experiences

1. Voices

Disembodied Voice: The voice will not come directly from a person, but rather will come from heaven or through some inanimate object, e.g.

the voice of God came to Moses disembodied through a burning bush (Exodus 3).

Authoritative: The voice will give a command to the recipient and compel him/her into action based on that experience, e.g. St Paul was compelled to go to Damascus and seek out Ananias to be converted based on the direction of Jesus' voice on the road (Acts of the Apostles 9).

Noetic: The voice will reveal some knowledge or information to the recipient which they would not have gained any other way, e.g. at Jesus' baptism the voice of God revealed that Jesus was in fact God's Son and that God was pleased with Jesus (Mark 1).

2. Visions

Corporeal: These visions are of a person in the appearance of flesh and can be interacted with though not everyone will necessarily be about to see them, e.g. St Bernadette saw Mary appear to her as a beautiful woman.

Imaginative: These visions appear within dreams and the recipient may receive particular knowledge or prophecy through it, e.g. Joseph was informed that Mary was pregnant through the power of the Holy Spirit and that he should not be afraid to marry her (Matthew 1).

Intellectual: These visions are more awareness of the presence of some being, being seen with the eye of the mind rather than in physical form, e.g. St Teresa of Avila claims she did not so much see Jesus, but was rather aware of him.

3. William James' Varieties (Acronym PINT)

Passive: All religious experiences must happen to the recipient in order to be religious; they cannot seek it out, e.g. the persons in the Bible and the mystics of Catholic history did not behave like witchdoctors who entered trances on purpose to receive divine knowledge. They were granted their experiences by God without seeking them out, e.g. Moses was a shepherd in Midian with no intention of returning to Egypt where he was wanted for murder, but experienced an encounter with God regardless in which he was directed to return to Egypt (Exodus 3).

Ineffable: All religious experiences must either be beyond human powers to describe or must be of such a nature as they go beyond everyday experiences, so are difficult to grasp and explain, e.g. St Teresa of Avila used creative language to help her describe what she was experiencing and admitted that aspects could not be explained.

Noetic: All religious experiences reveal some knowledge that the recipient could not gain by themselves; this may include the identity of the source of the experience, some theological knowledge, or even a deeper understanding of the relationship between God and the recipient, e.g. St Bernadette was told by Mary that she was the Immaculate Conception, a revelation that went on to form Catholic dogma about Mary's nature.

Transient: While the religious experience is a short encounter, the effects of the experience are long lasting and often involve conversion, e.g. St Paul was a staunch Jew persecuting the Christians, but following his encounter with Christ he converted to Christianity and became one of the great Apostles of the early Christian Church.

4. Richard Swinburne's Direct or Indirect Distinction

Public Ordinary: The interpretation of an ordinary encounter as something spiritual and meaningful, e.g. seeing the earth from orbit and realising how fragile life is.

Public Extraordinary: Being present during a miracle that goes beyond human powers to explain, e.g. witnessing a miraculous healing or one of the biblical miracles.

Private Describable: A **DIRECT** religious experience that can be fully described and understood, e.g. the interpretation of one of Joseph's dreams (Genesis 37).

Private Non-Describable: A **DIRECT** religious experience which cannot be fully described or understood, e.g. the experiences of St Teresa of Avila.

Private Non-Specific: An **INDIRECT** religious experience where the individual sees the world in a different way to help them come to an understanding of God, e.g. Antony Flew's reflection of DNA as proof of God's involvement in the design of the universe.

Veridicalness Of Religious Experience

William James

• Religious Experiences are **PSYCHOLOGICAL** phenomena; this means that they operate through the psyche. As such all people can have a religious experience; they are not unique to saints.

• Drugs and alcohol can open a recipient up to the divine. In the same way that Indian Yogi train their bodies to be more receptive to the divine, drugs and alcohol can lower the inhibitions of the individual to make them more receptive to the divine without instigating the encounter.

• The testimonies of Stephen Bradley and S. H. Hadley, as well as the biblical experiences and experiences of the Catholic mystics, all share the same **FOUR CHARACTERISTICS** of religious experience (acronym **PINT**), which show that they do in fact take place and affect the individuals' lives directly. If they were not genuine they would not have such impact on them to make them change their lives and convert to a new way of life.

Richard Swinburne's Two Principles

• The **PRINCIPLE OF CREDULITY** dictates that we accept the genuineness of the experiences we have unless we have a compelling reason not to, e.g. we do not believe in God for other reasons, we are drunk etc.

• The **PRINCIPLE OF TESTIMONY** dictates that we should accept the genuineness of other people's testimonies about religious experiences as we accept their testimonies about all other things; there is no difference about a religious experience and so we should not discriminate against religious experiences.

The Case Against Religious Experiences

The case against religious experiences comes from interpreting religious experiences as the product of influences on the **PSYCHE**, either due to direct **NEUROSIS** or as a result of physiological or sociological influences.

Psychological Neurosis

- **SIGMUND FREUD** argued that religion was itself a neurosis stemming from childhood neurosis. Belief in God was the **PROJECTION** of the need for an eternal **FATHER FIGURE** and as such had no basis in reality. This being the case, religious experience is nothing more than our need to manifest these neurotic ideas into justifications for our behaviour. This is all supported by Freud's research into the obsessive behaviour of patients at Salpêtriére hospital.

- **TIMOTHY LEARY** presented his findings that when mystical accounts were mixed with the accounts of drug users, the accounts were indistinguishable, which suggests that there is nothing distinctive about so-called 'religious' experiences. Rather, they are all products of the psyche.

- **JL MACKIE** argued that if religious experiences were in any way psychological, then those who accept that they have any authority at all are insufficiently critical of them. We should not accept the authority of these experiences if there is any way that they can be accounted for by the psyche itself.

Physiological Influences

- **HARLOW** described the character of Phineas Gage, a railway foreman, as agreeable and well-liked. Following the accident which resulted in a pole being thrust into his brain, his character changed markedly. This suggests that any physiological changes to the person that affect the brain in any way, will affect his behaviour and experiences. So, 'religious' experiences can be accounted for by **PHYSIOLOGICAL** changes in the person.

- **D. LANSBOROUGH** argued that St Paul may well have suffered temporal lobe epilepsy, which caused his temporary blindness and the voice he heard. The work of Professor **PERSINGER** into the effects of magnetism on the temporal lobes supports the theory that if the temporal lobes are affected, then the individual receives what appears to them to be vivid experiences of God or the devil.

- Many of the Catholic mystics, St Teresa of Avila, St Bernadette, St Faustina all suffered severe sicknesses prior to their mystical encounters. It is possible that either the sickness itself or any medication they received to combat it instigated the apparent 'religious' experience.

Sociological Influences

KARL MARX argued that a person's society directly affects the kinds of experiences they have. A Christian would encounter Jesus or Mary while a Hindu would encounter Vishnu. This is understandable as their societies dictate what they receive. Marx argued that religion was the **OPIUM** of the people. Much like Freud, he was cynical of the role of religion on people's behaviour and so he rejected it. For Marx, the Church was an institution that suppressed the masses so preventing them from flourishing, and so religious experience is part of that institution and propaganda that makes us fall into line. If we believe that God speaks to the leaders of the institution then we are more likely to obey them and do what we are told.

Strengths

- **FRIEDRICH SCHLEIERMACHER** argued that we all have a consciousness for the divine. This supports James' point that religious experiences are natural to us and that we are the ones who block it off by attaching ourselves to the mundane world.

- **RUDOLF OTTO** argued that religious experiences were the apprehension of the wholly 'other'. This would respond to Marx' challenge as the wholly other is **INEFFABLE** to us. We would have to translate it into language that we understood and that language would likely be influenced by our societies.

- **RICHARD SWINBURNE** argued that accounts of religious experiences were evidence in themselves. The **PRINCIPLE OF TESTIMONY** is used within scientific communities as evidence for theories and proofs. We should be able to use it to justify religious experiences as well.

- **WILLIAM ALSTON** argued that if we accept our senses with regards to ordinary experiences, there is no reason why we should suddenly stop relying on them in terms of religious experiences. This would be to practice a form of elitism.

The Catholic Church has authenticated 67 of the thousands of miracle claims at **LOURDES**. This authentication comes after decades of investigation by doctors into the claims of the recipients of the apparent miracles. If no other explanation can be found then the event is declared a miracle and the Church accepts it. If these are in fact miracles, they justify St Bernadette's religious experience as being genuine.

Weaknesses

- **SEXUAL REPRESSION** - When reading St Teresa of Avila's encounter with the Seraphim from a Freudian perspective, a lot of sexual imagery can be identified. This supports the argument that such experiences are in fact suppressed sexual tension disguised by neurosis and expressed as religious encounters.

- **OUTDATED VIEW OF MIND** - Modern understanding of the mind has allowed us to probe further into the way we gain knowledge and experiences. This allows us to be more critical about what we experience or think we are experiencing, including 'religious' experiences.

- **LACK OF RIGOUR** - Anthony O'Hear argued that we should apply checks when considering religious experiences:

  - Checking over time: Is the experience consistent over a period of time?

  - Checking with other senses: Do other senses support the initial encounter/experience?

  - Checking with other checkers: Do other people agree with the genuineness of the initial encounter?

If an experience cannot be checked then it is not scientifically **VERIFIED**.

While this does not mean that it is not real or genuine, it does mean that we cannot discuss the experience in the same way that we discuss other experiences.

Key Quotes

1. "At 14 I thought I saw the Saviour, by faith, in human shape, for about one second in the room, with arms extended, appearing to say to me, Come." Stephen Hadley from William James, Lecture IX on Conversion

2. "The sway of alcohol over mankind is unquestionably due to its power to stimulate the mystical faculties of human nature, usually crushed to earth by the cold facts and dry criticisms of the sober hour." William James, Lecture XVI and XVII on Mysticism

3. "Religion is comparable to a childhood neurosis." Sigmund Freud, The Future of an Illusion

4. "Suppose that drugs can induce experiences that are indistinguishable from religious ones, and that we can respect their reports. Do they shed any light, not (we now ask) on life, but on the nature of the religious life?" Huston Smith, Do Drugs have Religious Import?

5. "If it seems to a subject that X is present, then probably X is present; what one seems to perceive is probably so." Richard Swinburne, The Existence of God

Confusion To Avoid

The questions that surround the topic of religious experience all link to one central theme: the **AUTHORITY** of religious experiences over the recipient. If the religious experience is genuine then it has authority over the recipient. If it is not genuine then it should have no authority over them.

All challenges to religious experiences are ultimately challenges to the authority we should grant to the experience. If there is a **PSYCHOLOGICAL** influence then the experience is the product of the mind, not the workings of God. If there is a physiological influence, then the experience is the effect of sickness and so we should treat the patient, not deem their words divine.

We should always look for the line of debate and see how the question of authority of the experience is probed, and the influence the experience has on the recipient.

The **CHARACTERISTICS** of religious experiences do not answer this question by themselves. They should be used in conjunction with the arguments for the genuineness of the experiences and be used to show how religious experiences share characteristics and lead to positive lifestyles and conversions. If the experiences have similar attributes and lead to positive ends, it then supports the genuineness of them as religious experiences.

Possible Exam Questions

1. Assess the claim that religious experiences prove that God exists.

2. 'Religious experiences are nothing more than forms of psychological neurosis.' Discuss.

3. "Personal testimony can never be reliable evidence for God's existence". Discuss

4. Critically compare corporate religious experiences with individual experiences as a basis for belief in God.

The Problem of Evil

Key Terms

BENEVOLENCE - The characteristic that God loves us all

MORAL EVIL - The bad things that people do to others to cause suffering

NATURAL EVIL - The bad things that happen in nature that cause suffering

OMNIPOTENCE - The belief that God has all power to do anything

OMNISCIENCE - The belief that God knows all that is happening in the world

The Problem

The Problem of Evil and Suffering is often called the rock of atheism. It challenges the belief in God based on the classical Judaeo-Christian understanding that God is **BENEVOLENT**, all-powerful and all-knowing. It considers the revealed nature of God as incompatible with the existence of evil and suffering in the world, and so it is argued that this inconsistency proves that there can be no God.

• Epicurus' Version, The Inconsistent Triad

Is God able to prevent evil, but not able? Then he is not omnipotent.

Is God able, but not willing? Then he is **MALEVOLENT**.

Is he both able and willing? Then where does evil come from?

Is he neither able nor willing? Then why call him God?

• John Stuart Mill's Evil Nature

Mill argued that the evil and suffering within the natural world is enough to prove that there can be no benevolent designer of the world as no good being would permit such suffering within nature. Richard Dawkins used the **DIGGER WASP** to develop this point. The wasp paralyses the caterpillar to lay eggs inside it. When the eggs hatch, the caterpillar suffers and dies. This shows evil in nature.

• J.L. Mackie and H.L. McCloskey's Logical Problem of Evil

God is **OMNIPOTENT**. He is able to stop evil.

God is **OMNISCIENT**. He knows about the evil happening and he knew about it when he created.

God is **OMNIBENEVOLENT**. He does not want us to suffer.

Evil exists. People suffer though God knows about it, can and wants to prevent it.

• Peter Vardy's Five Types of Natural Evil

1. Natural disasters: earthquakes, tsunamis etc.

2. Diseases: cancer, diabetes etc.

3. Psychological illness: bipolar, multiple personality, autism etc.

4. Human frailty: pain during childbirth, colds and susceptibility to sickness.

5. Animal suffering: animals being killed by other animals.

Augustine's Theodicy

St Augustine argued that evil and suffering were not accountable to God, but rather to humanity. His theodicy was an attempt to demonstrate how we are ultimately responsible for the evil and suffering in the world.

What is Evil?

Augustine said that evil was a **PRIVATION** (a lack of something), not a force of its own. God created all things perfectly and evil is only a corruption of that good thing. In the same way that bad teeth are simply good teeth that have not been taken care of, evil in the world is good things that have not been nurtured and cared for, people not doing what they are supposed to be doing. So all that is evil came from God but when it did, it was still good.

The Fall of Adam and Eve

Augustine was not a **CREATIONIST** and so did not believe in the literal interpretation of Genesis 1 and 2, however, he used it to help teach how evil entered the world. It is through human disobedience that evil comes into the world. We disobey God and the ripple effects have consequences throughout creation.

Natural Evil

Augustine's appealing to Adam and Eve and how disobedience causes evil satisfactorily explains **MORAL** evil, but not **NATURAL** evil. For this, Augustine discussed how the Fall of Mankind rippled into the spiritual dimension, and so even angels fell from grace, and they cause natural evil in the world. This is the hierarchy of creation and the consequences of human disobedience.

The Eschatological Question

In the end (**ESCHATON**) God will judge us all based on our actions and how much we obeyed or disobeyed God.

Irenaeus' Theodicy

St Irenaeus presented an alternative theodicy to Augustine, which was easier to fit into the workings of everyday life. It explores evil as a part of God's creation, rather than an **UNWANTED CONSEQUENCE** which would lead to a questioning of God's power to prevent it.

Evil is good

Primarily, Irenaeus argued that evil, while bringing suffering, was not in itself a bad thing, but rather a **NECESSARY TOOL** to help us develop as human beings. We need suffering, risk and pain in order to make the right choices and develop as people. If we live a life without suffering we will never learn anything and will never value the **GOODNESS OF GOD**.

Adam and Eve

While Irenaeus was a **CREATIONIST**, he did not see it necessary to read Genesis in that way in order to learn from it. He argued that the example of Adam and Eve was just the first time human beings disobey God and are punished for it. We disobey God all the time and are punished and it is always the tempter who receives the greater punishment. However, Adam and Eve, in their infancy, could not have really been expected to know right from wrong, and so we can take comfort from that. God's punishment was a just punishment and it led to them learning and developing as it does for us.

Image and Likeness

Irenaeus' theodicy requires us to re-read the creation story slightly. While God created us in his **IMAGE**, in that we are capable of rational and moral thinking, He did not create us in his **LIKENESS**, but rather we need to live, learn and suffer in order to gain God's likeness.

Hick And Soul-Making

John Hick took Irenaeus' theodicy and developed it in order to make sense of it in a modern world. He argued that we are on earth for the purpose of **SOUL-MAKING**. That is, we need to learn and grow on earth and make our souls more like God. This happens through suffering. For this reason Christians see suffering as sometimes a good thing as it allows us to share Christ's suffering and make us more like Him.

Epistemic Distance

We are created at a distance from God, not a geographical distance (e.g. land and sky), but rather an **EPISTEMIC** one (episteme is Greek for knowledge), a **KNOWLEDGE GAP** that cannot be crossed on our terms. God has set this distance so humanity has awareness of God but not certainty. Humans are not born with the **INNATE KNOWLEDGE** of God's existence and have to seek God through faith.

Through our lives we must work on our souls in order to make them more perfect so that we can cross that distance. However, that can never be perfectly done in a lifetime, so eschatologically (at the end of time) God will cover that distance for us.

This leads to the (possibly unchristian) belief in universal salvation that in the end all will be saved.

Christ, the New Adam

Hick argued that Christ was the **NEW ADAM** and did what Adam could not do, resist temptation and ultimately show us how to be perfect. In fact, Christ tells us in Matthew to "be perfect, as your Father in heaven is perfect". This is our call and while we are not perfect on earth we suffer through **NATURAL** and **MORAL** evil as Christ suffered before us. However, through baptism we are working our souls to become more like Christ and be saved.

Strengths

Of Augustine

- Brian Davies supported Augustine's notion that evil is a **PRIVATION** rather than a substance in his example of bad deckchairs and sour grapes, all of which were examples of fallen objects. In fact, this model of good and evil marries directly with Aristotle's notion of goodness being the fulfilment of ones' final cause. If one does not, they are bad, if they cannot then they are corrupt.

- Alvin Plantinga argued in The Free Will Defence that Augustine was right that moral evil is accountable to human beings and that we cannot blame God, as it is better that God created free agents than obedient robots and where there is freedom there must be the freedom to disobey God.

Of Irenaeus and Hick

- This theodicy avoids the problems of a **PERFECT CREATION** going wrong which Augustine's theodicy faces. Since evil is part of God's creation there is no "problem of evil as such, as evil is part of the plan of God".

- This theodicy explains the importance of life on earth as a time of **DEVELOPMENT** and spiritual growth. This is absent in other theodicies and explains why we are here at all.

- Gottfried Leibniz argued that this must be the best of all possible worlds and the Irenaeus/Hick theodicy follows that model in that this is the only way the world could be. Without freedom we would be incapable of **GOODNESS** and without suffering we would be incapable of **GROWTH**.

Weaknesses

Of Augustine

- Friedrich Schleiermacher pointed out the **LOGICAL CONTRADICTION** in the idea that God created a perfect world which went wrong. Augustine did not address this. Grapes can go sour if you leave them out in the sun, but why would God leave us to go wrong - surely God's perfect nature would inform him of what will go wrong and he would address it?

- Since Augustine did not believe in the **LITERAL INTERPRETATION** of the Creation story or the story of the Fall of Adam, it makes no sense for him to rely on it so heavily in order to explain **NATURAL EVIL** in the world. The idea that all natural evil comes from the fallen angels who rebelled following the Fall of Adam seems far-fetched and inadequate to explain what we experience as tectonic plate movement (earthquake) and the various other types of natural evil that Peter Vardy identifies.

- The existence of **HELL** suggests that God knew his creation would disobey Him and that things would go 'wrong'. If God knew they would go this way, is it wrong? If not, and it was intended, then surely that justifies Irenaeus' theodicy.

Of Irenaeus and Hick

- Irenaeus' theodicy requires an **UNORTHODOX** reading of creation, in that we are meant to believe we are not made in God's image and likeness, which the Catholic Church maintains we are. Further, the principle of **UNIVERSAL SALVATION,** which Hick argues, is again counter to mainstream Christianity. The belief that we might go to hell if we are bad is a necessity if God is good and just and we are free. If we are all destined to go to heaven no matter what we do then there is no need to be 'good' on earth at all.

- This theodicy argues that we have suffering in order to learn and make our souls complete, but this does not justify the deaths of infants and even the unborn that had no chance to live or learn. Their deaths cannot help them to grow or make their souls. In fact, those who do evil to others often live longer than their victims, and so how are they learning?

- The **END** cannot morally justify the **MEANS**. Even if evil and suffering (the **MEANS**) did enable us to forge perfect souls (the **END**, there is so much evil and suffering that surely God would be able to find another way, e.g. a life simulator where people did not actually suffer.

Key Quotes

1. "Is God willing to prevent evil, but unable to do so? Then he is not omnipotent. Is God able to prevent evil, but is not willing to? Then he is malevolent. Is God able to prevent evil and willing to? Then why is there evil?" Epicurus

2. "'Evil comes from God'. It was obvious to me that things which are liable to corruption are good. If there were no good in them there would be nothing capable of being corrupted." Augustine

3. "All of nature is good, since the Creator of all nature is supremely good. But nature is not supremely and immutably good, as is the Creator of it. When a thing is corrupted, its corruption is an evil because it is a privation of the good." Augustine

4. "Nearly all the things which men are hanged or imprisoned for doing to one another are nature's everyday performances." John Stuart Mill

5. "Here it can be shown, not that religious beliefs lack rational support, but that they are positively irrational, that several parts of the essential theological doctrine are inconsistent with one another." J.L. Mackie

6. "Virtues resulting from suffering are intrinsically more valuable than virtues created within a person, ready made without effort on his own part." John Hick

7. "Humanity is created at an epistemic distance from God in order to come freely to know and love their Maker; and that they are at the same time created." John Hick

Confusion To Avoid

St Augustine uses the **FALL** of Adam and Eve to explain human **FREE WILL** and wickedness. In fact, he argued that **ORIGINAL SIN** alone was enough to damn all humanity to hell. However, Augustine was not a Creationist; he did not believe that the Creation stories of Genesis were intended to be literally read. Conversely, St Irenaeus' theodicy teaches it does not matter if Adam and Eve were real, as every time we disobey God we are repeating the sin of Adam and Eve, but he was in fact a **CREATIONIST**.

Possible Exam Questions

1. 'There is no solution to the problem of evil and suffering.' Discuss.

2. Assess the success of John Hick's argument for soul-making as a development of Irenaeus' theodicy.

3. Assess which logical or evidential aspects of the problem of evil pose the greatest challenge to belief.

4. Critically assess whether it is possible to defend monotheism in the face of the existence of evil.

Book 2
Religious Thought Year 1

OCR Revision Guide (New Spec)

Daniella Dunsmore

Augustine - Human Nature

Background & Influences

Augustine was influenced in his thought on human nature by:

1. MANICHEES – each person has a good and bad soul. We escape wrong-doing by using our reason and following positive role models.

2. NEOPLATONISM – Plotinus. Good and evil are not distinct realms. Only the Form of the Good exists.

3. BIBLE - St Paul's Letter to the Romans – God's grace was necessary.

At AS and A level, you will need to explain and evaluate Augustine's view on human relationships pre-and post-Fall; Original Sin and its effects on the will and human societies, and God's grace.

Key Terms

AKRASIA - paradox of voluntarily choosing to do something we know is against our best interests.

CARITAS - 'generous love', a love of others and of the virtues.

CONCORDIA - human friendship.

CONCUPISCENCE - uncontrollable desire for physical pleasures and material things.

CUPIDITAS - 'selfish love', a love of worldly things and of selfish desires.

DOCTRINE - means 'teaching'. The official teaching of the Roman Catholic Church.

ECCLESIA - heavenly society, in contrast with earthly society.

GRACE - theologically, God's free and unearned love for humankind, embodied in the sacrifice of Jesus on the cross.

MANICHEES - humans have two souls. One desires God, the other desires evil. Evil is not caused by God, but by a lower power. The body is evil and sinful.

NEOPLATONISM - influenced by Plato; the body belongs to the realm of flesh and is necessarily imperfect.

ONTOLOGICAL - the being or nature of existence.

OPTIMISTIC VIEW OF HUMAN NATURE - humans are only immoral because of poor education or psychological fault.

ORIGINAL SIN - Christian belief that despite being made in God's image the human condition means we cannot reach this state.

PELAGIANS - Christians who believed humans could overcome personal sin with free will. No universal guilt.

PESSIMISTIC VIEW OF HUMAN NATURE - humans are naturally ego-centric and violent for the sake of survival.

POST-LAPSARIAN - the world after the fall of Adam and Eve.

SIN - disobeying God's will and commands.

SUMMUM BONUM - he highest, most supreme good.

THE FALL - the biblical event in which Adam and Eve disobeyed God's command and ate the fruit from the forbidden tree in the Garden of Eden.

WILL - the part of human nature that makes free choices.

Human Relationships Pre And Post-Fall

The **ORIGINAL SIN** of Adam and Eve ruined the relationship humankind could have had with God.

Augustine teaches that this '**original sin**' passes on through generations **SEMINALLY** (by sperm)**,** making human nature flawed. However, Jesus' death on the cross was seen as a **SACRIFICE**, paying the price of sin, meaning Christians could be saved through God's **GRACE**.

Christian tradition understands humanity in terms of its relationship with God. This is threefold:

1. Humans are **created** by God.

2. Humans are '**fallen**' in nature.

3. Humans can be **redeemed**.

Pre-Fall

- Shared nature of **IMAGO DEI** means humans can all be seen to be equal.

- The **SECOND GENESIS** account of creation shows humans as **SPECIAL** in God's creation but simultaneously part of the natural world. God breathes life into man. God animates man - different to **PLATO'S** notion of the soul trapped by the body.

- Once created, humans are not programmed to act in a certain way. They have a set of rules to follow e.g. multiply, be stewards, do not eat from the forbidden tree. They have potential to be both obedient and disobedient – made with **FREE CHOICE** and made perfectly.

- Humans were made with a **DUTY OF OBEDIENCE** to God's demands and existed harmoniously, observing their duties to other living creatures.

- The state of perfection **PRE-FALL** meant that the human will, the body, and reason cooperated with each other entirely.

- Humans are naturally sociable and friendship is the highest form of this. **CONCORDIA** is used to describe Adam and Eve's relationship **PRE-FALL**. Adam and Eve were not just living together, but were living in a state of the very best of all possible human relationships.

Post-Fall

- The will can be driven by **CUPIDITAS** or **CARITAS**.

- After the first free decision to disobey, Adam and Eve became aware of their sexual bodies. Through **REASON** the will knows what is good but is often motivated by **CONCUPISCENCE** rather than by goodness. Concupiscence can distract from God and break up friendship.

- Post-Fall, the will became in conflict with itself and could lead to freely choosing what we know to go against our best interests. This is known as **AKRASIA** (weakness of will).

- Augustine used his own example of a beautiful, chaste woman – **CONTINENCE**. Not even she could convince Augustine to embrace celibacy – **"Lord, make me chaste, but not yet!"**.

- The battle with sin cannot be won without turning to Christ, as shown in Paul's Letter to the **ROMANS,** and the extracts from **CONFESSIONS**.

Original Sin - Effects On The Human Will & Society

Augustine and Pelagius

- Sin is an **ONTOLOGICAL CONDITION** of Human Existence. We might appear **VIRTUOUS**, but no one is truly good.

- **PELAGIUS** - while Adam set a poor example, it was not the one that we had to follow and we could, if we tried, live morally.

- Augustine disagreed with Pelagius - human efforts alone were not enough – we need God's **GRACE** and **CHRIST**.

- The inherited **ORIGINAL SIN** causes human selfishness and a lack of free will; plus a lack of stability and corruption in all human societies.

Human Selfishness & Free Will

- The **FALL** left the will divided. Paul's Letter to the **ROMANS** described Paul's struggle between his **SELFISH DESIRES** and his **SPIRITUAL INCLINATIONS**, (see Romans 7).

- Paul speaks of Christians as 'forgiven sinners' through their faith and this partially explains how Christians still behave wrongly even after accepting salvation. Paul implies that the release from sin will come with death of the body.

- **SEXUAL LUSTS** are evidence of sinful **CUPIDITAS**. Augustine said that even within marriage, a couple should take a vow of **CELIBACY** once they had had enough children. People should live plainly and simply to devote themselves to God.

- In '**On the Good of Marriage**' - the physical delight of sex in marriage should be distinguished from libido (misuse of impulse). It is 'pardonable' to enjoy sex without the intention of procreation. Like **ARISTOTLE** and **PAUL**, he stressed **'mutual obligation'**.

- In '**On Free Will**' Augustine suggests that free will makes it possible to use reason to aspire to the Good (human flourishing) by living virtuously. This is **PLATONIC**.

- However, human reason cannot overcome the punishments of the Fall. Sin is involuntary and we cannot help but fall into wrong-doing. We prefer to do wrong because our souls are 'chained' by sin. Neither living **ASCETICALLY** (nun/ monk) or opting for a **CHASTE** life could enable the will to be free and strong enough to resist

CONCUPISCENCE in its various forms.

Lack of Stability & Corruption in Human Societies

A forceful political authority was needed to help society function.

The Bible teaches that humans are appointed to rule over other species, but not each other. **PRE-FALL**, leaders in society were **SHEPHERDS** not kings (**City of God**).

'Earthly peace' is a material and not a spiritual aim. **EARTHLY PEACE** is the best sort of life sinful people can aim for but even this is corrupted. The measures needed for earthy peace (e.g. self-restraint) are only necessary because of the Fall.

Commitment to the common good is a consequence of sinful human nature and not, as **AQUINAS** would say, a **MORAL VIRTUE**. We are **'pilgrims in a foreign land'** – we need to live as earthly people out of necessity; but should keep focussed on the heavenly destination, the **'City of God'**.

This **'heavenly society'** is called **ECCLESIA** and is 'perfect living'. Heavenly society is known only through death and the **GRACE** of God and is poorly and partially reflected in the **earthly society.**

God's Grace

- The rebellious will and **SIN** could only be overcome by God's grace, made possible through Jesus' sacrifice. Only then can the supreme good (**SUMMUM BONUM**) be achieved.

- Augustine's teaching on God's grace laid the foundation for Catholic confession – the Sacrament of **RECONCILIATION**.

- The Christian doctrine of **ELECTION** teaches that salvation is possible because God chooses to redeem humans first. God has elected those he knows will answer his love and be restored to paradise. The elected are assisted by the **HOLY SPIRIT**

- Contradicts New Testament suggestion that 'all' are saved – unless this means that God saves across races and cultures (see 2 Peter 3:9).

- **JOHN 3** led Augustine to believe that heaven could not be reached by anyone deliberately denying baptism. Unbaptised babies could be condemned to hell. This is not as a result of choice – infants do not 'choose' to deny baptism.

- Faith in God's love and an acknowledgement of the failings of human nature are essential on the path to **EUDAIMONIA** - "unless you believe, you will not understand" (Isaiah 7:9).

- John 3 showed Augustine that **FAITH** and **BAPTISM** together were needed as human nature is **ONTOLOGICALLY** flawed.

God's grace is understood as:

- God's **LOVE** and **MERCY**; that He is capable of reaching the heart and will of a person and can give moral guidance to the lives of Christians; something that cannot be deserved by any human on their own merit.

- The quality that enables a person's soul to **RECOGNISE** when it has offended God and when it should praise God.

- Capable of **TRANSFORMING** the human will so that it is capable of obeying God.

- Capable of **OVERCOMING** human pride and can calm the soul with forgiveness and hope.

- **VISIBLE** in Christ's sacrifice and in the gift of the Holy Spirit working in the Church.

MNEMONIC: Lovely Mary Really Transformed Our Vase

Happiness in this earthly life is temporary. Plato's **FORM OF THE GOOD** is similar to Augustine's understanding of God's goodness in Christianity. The **SUMMUM BONUM** is a state of eternal happiness. It cannot be earned and is the highest goal one can aim for – achievable only through god's grace.

Strengths

- Close to the reality that people often find themselves **tempted** by material goods, yet wanting to do right.

- **Augustine** draws attention to the dangers of uncontrolled sexual behaviour – see how societies restrict it. Recognising human imperfection might lead to more moral progress.

- The **Pelagian** belief that human effort could bring about perfection was optimistic and doomed to fail. Augustine's teaching of our imperfect natures allows us to have genuine hope in God's grace.

- The body and human reason can be **in tension** with the body being willing, but the will not so. This supports the view that sex must have been under the control of the human will pre-Fall. Sex did not come about because of **the Fall**; but rather, was affected by it.

- Other schools of thought suggest a **single human nature**. E.g. Buddhism – human nature is characterised by the impermanency of all things and suffering because of attachment and desires. Evolutionary biology suggests the single human nature that is driven by survival instinct.

Weaknesses

- **Original sin** as 'ontologically present' is difficult to reconcile with belief in a benevolent God. Human nature is not fundamentally corrupt! **Rousseau** argued that humans are, by nature, good and inclined to defend the weak and work for a better society. **Rousseau** and **Locke** later asserted the 'blank state' (**'tabula rasa'**). We are born with – neither a good nor evil state, but readiness to make free choices..

- **Sartre**, an **existentialist**, suggests we have the freedom to create our own nature – rather than being born condemned.

- **Predestination/ Election** – if our fates are already decided, what responsibility can we have for our moral actions? With no real freedom, what incentive do we have to become better?

- **Richard Dawkins** - while the Christian concept of 'original sin' does not wholly contradict evolutionary biology, the idea that human nature could be restored through the death of Jesus is sado-masochistic!

- **Freud** (1856-1939) – one of the founders of **psychoanalysis** – wrote that sex is an important and natural aspect of human development; whereas **Augustine's** link between sex and transmission of sin makes sex only necessary for reproduction. Sex can transmit human disorders but sin is not one of these! Rather than a product of sexual intercourse, sin is a product of our environment (family, religion, education, or lack thereof). Augustine fails to acknowledge the natural enjoyment of sex within marriage.

- **Steven Pinker (psychologist)** supports **Dawkins**. **God's Grace** is not needed as our actions as rational, autonomous beings can succeed and allow us responsibility.

Possible Exam Questions

1. Assess the view that Augustine's teaching on human nature is too pessimistic

2. Critically assess the view that Christian teaching on human nature can only make sense if the Fall did actually happen

3. "Augustine's teaching on human nature is more harmful than helpful". Discuss.

4. How convincing is Augustine's teaching about the Fall and Original Sin?

5. Critically assess Augustine's analysis of human sexual nature.

Key Quotes

1. "For they would not have arrived at the evil act if an evil will had not preceded it". (Augustine, city of God).

2. "I do not understand what I do. For what I want to do I do not do, but what I hate I do". (St. Paul's Letter to the Romans)

3. "In vain did I delight in Your law after the inner man, when another law in my members warred against the law of my mind." (Augustine, Confessions).

4. "No one can enter the kingdom of God unless they are born of water and the Spirit". (John 3)

5. "Whoever believes in him is not condemned, but whoever does not believe stands condemned already." (John 3)

6. "What kind of ethical philosophy is it that condemns every child, even before it is born, to inherit the sin of a remote ancestor?" (Richard Dawkins, God Delusion)

Death and the Afterlife

Background And Influences

Jesus' teachings rooted in **JEWISH TRADITION** and **ESCHATOLOGY** of his time. Influenced by the teaching of the **PHARISEES** who were influenced by **GREEK** notions of the soul and immortality.

Jesus taught his life was a **SACRIFICE** for sin and his death would bring about a **NEW KINGDOM**.

Some believed the 'new Kingdom' to be **IMMINENT.** Different beliefs about the Kingdom of God include whether it is **an actual place, a spiritual state, or a symbol of moral life.**

At AS level, you will need to show knowledge and evaluation of Christian teaching on Heaven, Hell, and Purgatory, and Christian teaching on Election.

Key Terms

ESCHATOLOGY - discussion of the end-times, including battle between good and evil and God's judgement of the world.

PHARISEES - influential religious leaders at the time of Jesus. Differed to other traditional Jews at the time (e.g. Sadducees) because the Pharisees did believe in angels and bodily resurrection.

MARTYR - someone killed for their religious faith.

PAROUSIA - Greek for 'arrival'. Christ's 'second coming'.

BOOK OF REVELATION - the final book in the New Testament. Contains powerful visions of the end-time, heaven, and hell.

KINGDOM OF GOD - God's rule in this world and the next.

GOSPEL OF MATTHEW - shows interest in the Jewish Law and its relationship with Jesus' new law.

HADES and **GEHENNA**: Hades – for departed spirits awaiting judgement; Gehenna - a symbol for punishment of the wicked.

SHEOL - Old Testament equivalent to Hades.

SADDUCEES - political contemporaries of Jesus. Rejected belief in afterlife and bodily resurrection.

MARANATHA - Aramaic – 'O Lord, come!' 1 Cor 16:22 (once in NT)

MILLENARIANISM - idea that Christ will return and rule on Earth for 1000 years followed by final Judgement. Based on Revelation 20:2-5.

PURGATORY - where those who have died in a state of grace continue to seek forgiveness and receive punishment awaiting Final Judgement.

PARABLE - short story or saying which communicates a moral, spiritual or religious message.

MORTAL SIN - sin deliberately in defiance of God's law.

VENIAL SIN - errors of judgement, can be forgiven.

BEATIFIC VISION - final and perfect human state of everlasting happiness and knowledge of God; achieved post-mortem for the righteous in heaven.

PREDESTINATION - Christian teaching that God chooses and guides some people to eternal salvation.

PERDITION - eternal punishment - hell, purgatory, damnation.

DIVINE DECREE - God's ruling.

DOUBLE PREDESTINATION - God elects the righteous for Heaven and condemns sinners to Hell

WESTMINSTER CONFESSION OF FAITH - 1646, sets out principle beliefs of Reformed Christianity.

SINGLE PREDESTINATION - God predestines some to heaven but the wicked elect Hell for themselves.

APOKATASTASIS - Hell is not eternal. Eschatological goal of cosmos is perfection to pre-Fall state.

Christian Teaching On Heaven, Hell And Purgatory

1. Heaven, hell, and purgatory as **ACTUAL PLACES**.

2. Heaven, hell, and purgatory as not places, but **SPIRITUAL STATES** that a person experiences as part of their spiritual journey after death.

3. Heaven, hell, and purgatory as **SYMBOLS** of a person's spiritual and moral life on earth and not places or states after death.

Ideas About The Kingdom Taught By Jesus

1. A present moral and spiritual state. A call for moral and spiritual reform now. Jesus' healing miracles seem to fulfil prophecies of Isaiah and Jesus presents the Kingdom of God as if it has already begun. This 'nowness' is seen in his parables and examples of how to reach out to the lowly.

2. A future redeemed state. Made possible through Jesus' death and resurrection.

3. A place of punishment and justice. Where the wicked will suffer and those who suffered will prosper.

Problems

1. PAROUSIA seems delayed. One of the earliest prayers recorded is for the Parousia – **maranatha** (1 Corinthians 16:22). Jesus emphasises the mystery surrounding this date.

2. WHERE is this new Kingdom? On earth or in heaven (or both)?

3. FINAL JUDGEMENT v INDIVIDUAL – which is more important? Rich man and Lazarus implies judgement is immediate (Luke 16:13-31). Others suggest it happens at the end-time.

4. PURGATORY is not a term used in the New Testament. Arose out of fairness to allow people time to prepare for God's final judgement and as a result of ambiguity surrounding personal and final judgement.

Eschatological Teaching

1. **PAROUSIA** (second coming of Christ)

2. **RESURRECTION** (at the last day a 'trumpet will sound', 1 Cor. 15)

3. **JUDGEMENT** (Matthew 25 - sheep and goats separated)

Hell - Different Ideas

SPIRITUAL STATE: **Origen** (184-253 AD) – a person's interior anguish separated from God, where "each sinner kindles his own fire ...and our own vices from its fuel" (Cited in Wilcockson & Campbell, 2016, p. 273).

CONSCIENCE: **Gregory of Nyssa** (335-395 AD) – a guilty conscience when before Christ leads to judgement and torture of Hell.

DANTE (1265-1321): Hell is antithesis to Heaven – "through me the way into the woeful city, through me the way to eternal pain, through me the way to the lost people...abandon every hope, ye that enter" (Dante Divine Comedy cited in Wilcockson & Campbell, 2016, p. 274).

SYMBOL OF ALIENATION: **Paul Tillich** (1886-1965) – hell-type language has a place. Traditional metaphors are reinterpreted as spiritual and psychological descriptions of human alienation: "heaven and hell must be taken seriously as metaphors for the polar ultimates in the experience of the divine" (Tillich, P, Systematic theology III, 1964, p. 446, cited in Wilcockson & Campbell, 2016, p. 275).

HELL AS ETERNAL SEPARATION: Catholic teaching – Hell is real eternal for those who have committed mortal sins.

Purgatory

1. A **Catholic** and **Protestant** way of extending the opportunity for repentance beyond this life, even though there is no clear representation of this in the New Testament, just one hint **1 PETER 3:19**. "When made alive, Jesus went to preach to the spirits in prison".

1. Foretaste of Heaven and Hell – **Ambrose** (340 -397 AD).

2. Probationary school – **Origen**.

3. Redemption of the whole of creation – **Gregory of Nyssa** – purgatory has a **PURIFYING PURPOSE** for all people to help God complete his purpose of restoring all creation.

Dante's Vision

- For souls who believed in Christ and repented before death; a place for positive **PURGING** since one cannot sin in purgatory.

- The soul ascends terrains of mountain, the goal of which is **BEATIFIC VISION**. Soul is driven by love and later on, reason. An allegory for how life should be lived on earth too with its various temptations before the goal of salvation.

Catholic Teaching On Purgatory

- Ideas of **CLEANSING** of sins by fires implies that forgiveness is possible in this and in the next life.

- A stage in soul's journey to salvation.

- Prayers for the dead pre-dates Christianity – **JUDAS MACCABEUS** (2nd C BC) – prayed that the souls of the dead should be freed from sin.

- St John **CHRYSOSTOM** writes: "All who die in God's grace and friendship, but still imperfectly purified, are indeed assured of their eternal salvation; but after death they undergo purification, so as to achieve the holiness necessary to enter the joy of heaven".

Hick - The Intermediary State

- Some Protestants reject **PURGATORY** on the grounds of lack of Biblical evidence.

- Others are persuaded of the continued journey of the soul after death.

- **JOHN HICK** says that the gap between our imperfection at the end of this life, and the state of perfect **SOUL-MAKING** process begun on Earth.

Heaven

- The **RESTORATION** of the whole of creation, not just the individual's relationship with God.

- **DANTE** – Heaven is beyond words. Rational soul strives for ultimate good and Divine harmony. God as source of love and governor of universe is experienced.

- **CATHOLIC TEACHING** – Heaven is a "state of supreme, definitive happiness" (Cited in Wilcockson & Campbell, 2016, p. 278). God is wholly revealed in **BEATIFIC VISION**. A community of immortal souls in communion with Christ and obedient.

Election - Who Will Be Saved?

Limited Election

- Only a few Christians will be saved.

- 'Limited atonement' – Christ died only for the sins of the Elect.

Unlimited Election

- All people called to salvation, not all are saved.

- 'Unlimited atonement' – Christ died for the sins of the whole world.

Universalist Belief (Apokatastasis - restoration)

- All people will be saved - required by God's goodness and love.

- A requirement of human free will – we should all be able to reach salvation.

- Upbringing should not exclude people from reconciliation with God.

JOHN HICK – The God preached about by Jesus is not one who excludes. Jesus' resurrection is a triumph over death, not eternal damnation.

KARL BARTH - CALVINIST and not strictly universalist but helpful. God is both elected and elector and it is not for humans to speculate on the mystery of salvation.

Predestination

Election and Predestination

- **AUGUSTINE** – salvation only possible because of God's grace. God's grace is **unprompted but freely given.**

- God calls all to salvation but knows from the beginning that only some are eligible for a place in Heaven (**ELECT**).

- Some are not capable of receiving God's grace and are predestined for Hell (**PERDITION**).

Single And Double Predestination

- **SINGLE**: God elects only those for Heaven

- **DOUBLE**: God elects for both Heaven and Hell.

- **ANTELAPSARIAN DECREE**: God decreed the elect at the moment of creation, pre-Fall.

- **POSTLAPSARIAN DECREE:** God decreed the elect post-Fall.

Calvin

1. God **FOREKNOWS** what will happen but His will is hidden.

2. As Human knowledge is **LIMITED**, God's revelation takes this into account.

3. **GOD WILLS** his grace and mercy for all kinds of people.

4. Even if God has chosen particular individuals, **CHRISTIAN DUTY** is to spread God's words to all kinds of people.

5. Both the **ELECT** and the **NON-ELECT** have a duty to act morally.

Thomas Aquinas And Catholicism

- Aquinas – the Fall did not wipe out human freedom.

- Catholic Church – **SINGLE** predestination.

- "God predestines no one to go to Hell; for this, a wilful turning away from God (a mortal sin) is necessary, and persistence in it until the end" (Catechism of the Catholic Church para. 1037).

Parable Of Sheep & Goats (Matthew 25)

• **Reversal of expectation**. 'Righteous' would have been thought to have meant those who observed Jewish law. Jesus teaches that religious observance is not enough to earn a place in God's Kingdom. One must pursue justice for the marginalised without thinking of heavenly reward.

• **Reward is for ALL who pursue justice**, not just Christians. The God of love rewards all of good will.

• Jesus' **own ministry** of healing and serving the oppressed is reflected in his list of acts that would be rewarded.

• **Challenge to traditional teaching** that you are only obligated to help those in the same social and religious group as yourself. "Just as you did to one of the least of these who are members of my family, you did it to me" (Matthew 25:40).

Q. DOES GOD'S JUDGEMENT TAKE PLACE IMMEDIATELY AFTER DEATH OR AT THE END OF TIME?

AFTER DEATH	END OF TIME
Parable of the Rich Man and Lazarus (Luke 16:19-31)	Irenaeus
Jesus' words at crucifixion (Luke 23:42-43)	When God's plan for creation comes to conclusion.
NB placement of comma before or after 'today' makes a big difference!	Whole nations, as well as every person judged.

Q. ARE HELL AND HEAVEN ETERNAL?

YES	NO
Aquinas e.g. Beatific Vision – a timeless moment.	Would a benevolent God eternally damn and punish?
Accords with Biblical teaching - Matthew 25.	Hick – eternal Hell conflicts with Christian notions of God.
Augustine – we all deserve eternal punishment in Hell.	Can any human sin be so bad as to warrant eternal punishment?

Q. IS HEAVEN THE TRANSFORMATION AND PERFECTION OF THE WHOLE OF CREATION?

YES	NO
Revelation 21:1	Barth – not in a single event but in resurrection, Pentecost etc.
Parousia	Perfection/ transformation is in the hands of Christians today.

Q. IS PURGATORY A STATE THROUGH WHICH EVERYONE GOES?

YES	NO
Catholic. "Each man receives his eternal retribution in his immortal soul at the very moment of his death, in a particular judgment that refers his life to Christ: either entrance into the blessedness of heaven - through a purification or immediately, - or immediate and everlasting damnation". (Catechism 1021))	Less popular in Protestant doctrine. John Wesley, for example, taught that the perfection we seek in life is completed at "the instant of death, the moment before the soul leaves the body" (Brief Thoughts on Christian Perfection, 1767).
Necessary for souls to be fully purified to enter God's presence.	Jesus' death and resurrection saved us from sin, allowing immediate presence of God.

Possible Exam Questions

1. To what extent can belief in the existence of purgatory be justified?

2. "Heaven is not a place but a state of mind." Discuss.

3. "Without the reward of Heaven Christians would not behave well." Discuss.

4. To what extent is the Parable of the Sheep and the Goats in Matthew 25 only about Heaven and Hell?

5. Assess the view that there is no last judgement; each person is judged by God at the moment of their death.

6. "Purgatory is the most important Christian teaching about the afterlife." Discuss.

Key Quotes

1. "The time is fulfilled, and the kingdom of God is near" (Mark 1:14)

2. "But if it is by the finger of God that I cast out the demons, then the kingdom of God has come to you" (Luke 11:20).

3. "Then the eyes of the blind shall be opened, and the ears of the deaf unstopped; then the lame shall leap like a deer, the tongue of the speechless sing for joy" (Isaiah 35:5-6).

4. "Anyone whose name was not found written in the book of life was thrown into the lake of fire" (Revelation 20:15).

5. "But about that day and hour no one knows, neither the angels of heaven, nor the Son, but only the Father" (Matthew 24:36).

6. "If what has been built on the foundation survives, the builder will receive a reward. If the work is burned the builder will suffer loss; the builder will be saved, but only as through fire" (1 Corinthians 3:14-15).

7. "God has not rejected his people whom he foreknew" (Romans 11:2).

8. "This is good, and is acceptable in the sight of God our Saviour, who desires all men to be saved and come to the knowledge of truth" (1 Timothy 2:4).

9. "All who die in God's grace and friendship, but still imperfectly purified, are indeed assured of their eternal salvation; but after death they undergo purification, so as to achieve the holiness necessary to enter the joy of heaven." (Catechism 1030)

10. "The Church gives the name Purgatory to this final purification of the elect, which is entirely different from the punishment of the damned. The tradition of the Church, by reference to certain texts of Scripture, speaks of a cleansing fire". (Catechism 1031)

Knowledge of God

Background & Influences

NATURAL THEOLOGY is concerned with demonstrating God's existence. Some have assumed God's existence to be logically true. God revealed in the natural world seems removed from Biblical ideas of God as love.

REVEALED THEOLOGY suggests that God allows himself to be known in a special way e.g. in Jesus Christ or the example of the Prophet Muhammad (PBUH).

Problem: God is uniquely different to any other object. Natural theology would have to accept this. Revealed theology seems to neglect reason.

What is 'true knowledge'?

1.   **Incorrigible facts** (verifiable)

2.   **Wisdom** – understanding life and what gives it value

3.   **Knowledge** of God as the source of life

At AS and A level, you will need to show understanding and evaluation of natural knowledge of God's existence as an innate human sense of the Divine, and as seen in the order of Creation; and revealed knowledge of God's existence through faith and God's grace, and in Jesus Christ.

Key Terms

NATURAL THEOLOGY - God can be known through reason and observation of the natural world.

REVEALED THEOLOGY - God can only be known when he lets himself be known e.g. through prophets, scripture, prayer.

POINT OF CONTACT - God's revelation in the world, first step in humans knowing God as redeemer.

SENSUS DIVINITATIS - Latin used by Calvin to mean a 'sense of God'.

DUPLEX COGNITIO DOMINI - 'two-fold knowledge of God' – Calvin's distinction of knowing God as Creator and as Redeemer.

ARGUMENT FROM DESIGN - we must infer a designer (God) of the universe from the universe's complexities.

PRINCIPLE OF ACCOMMODATION - God reveals himself through creation in ways that limited human minds can best understand.

SI INTEGER STETISSET ADAM - Latin used by Calvin meaning 'if Adam had remained upright' – referring to the Fall.

REGENERATION - Christian understanding of the process of renewal, restoration, and recreation linked with baptism and other sacraments of the Church.

TRINITARIAN VIEW OF GOD - central to the Christian teaching that God is one but reveals Himself as three 'persons': Father, son, Holy Spirit.

IMMANENCE - 'being part of' – refers to God's participation in all aspects of the world and universe.

ATHEOLOGICAL OBJECTOR - term used by Plantinga to refer to those who reject all theological claims.

FIDEISM - Revelation is essential for the human mind to know anything certain about the existence of God or nature.

THOUGHT EXPERIMENT - like a scientific experiment but in the mind, without instruments. Aim: to discover truths about the real world through reasoned reflection.

Natural Knowledge Of God's Existence As An Innate Sense Of The Divine

Sensus Divinitatis

As all humans are made in God's **IMAGE** - they have an inbuilt capacity and desire to know God, including:

- **Human openness** to beauty and goodness as aspects of God

- **Human intellectual ability** to reflect on and recognise God's existence

Both **CALVIN** and the **CATECHISM** of the Catholic Church agree that knowledge of God is **INNATE** (we are born with it).

CALVIN called this innate knowledge of God **SENSUS DIVINITATIS**.

SEMEN RELIGIONIS – seed of religion – human inclination to carry out religious practices e.g. rituals and prayer.

Innate Knowledge

- **UNKNOWN GOD** – **Acts 17:16-34** – Paul tries to convince Athenians they are worshipping the true God, even if they do not know this.

- **UNIVERSAL CONSENT** – **Cicero, Calvin** – so many people believe in a God/ gods that there MUST exist a god!

- **HUMANS ARE RELIGIOUS** – religious rituals and meditations are so universal that **"one may well call man a religious being"** (Catechism 28).

Sense of Beauty & Moral Goodness

The foundations of knowledge of God in Protestant and Catholic Christianity.

- **NATURAL LAW** – particularly Catholicism – all humans have an innate awareness of justice and fairness, even if ill-informed. Aquinas calls this innate orientation to the good **SYNDERESIS**.

- **CONSCIENCE** – particularly important to Calvin's ideas about knowledge of God. Conscience is God-given to humans made **imago dei** with '**Joint knowledge'** between us and God. God's presence gives us the sense of moral judgement within us.

Human Intellectual Ability To Reflect On & Recognise God's Existence

Seen in example of **Thomas Aquinas' FiIVE WAYS** - God as **UNCAUSED CAUSER** who sustains all things.

Best knowledge we have here is that God exists differently to other beings.

Consider: how can we be **SURE** that this is God?

Natural Knowledge in the Order of Creation

- The idea that what can be known of God can be seen in the apparent design and purpose of nature

- **CALVIN – duplex cognitio Domini** – two-fold knowledge of God as **CREATOR** and as **REDEEMER**.

- As Creator, the **ORDER** and **DESIGN** in the universe are strong sources of revelation.

- **PRINCIPLE OF ACCOMMODATION** – Calvin's explanation that human minds are finite and therefore cannot know God through **REASON** alone. Hence, God manifests himself through creation.

- What we know of God through creation is "a sort of **MIRROR** in which we can contemplate God, who is otherwise invisible" (John Calvin: Institutes I.V.1).

Purpose

- **William Paley** – watch analogy; God as infinitely powerful maker.

- Challenge- nature seems more cruel than beautiful. Darwin's challenge of evolution too.

- **PROCESS THEOLOGY** developed in response to challenges to Paley's argument and influenced by the principle of **QUANTUM UNCERTAINTY**. Proposes that God works **WITH** the natural processes, not separate to them. Each individual moment is an end in itself – the universe as a whole is not working towards a particular end.

- **GOD IS KNOWABLE** – in contrast with ideas of classical theology. God loves and suffers with creation, helping each aspect to achieve its potential. God's participation in nature is revealed in every moment of creation. Process theology - there is no clear difference between natural and revealed theology.

Revealed Knowledge of God's Existence

As humans are sinful and have finite minds, natural knowledge is not sufficient to gain full knowledge of God; knowledge of God is possible through:

- **FAITH** - "Happy are those that do not see yet believe". (John 20:29)

- **GRACE** as God's gift of knowledge of himself through the Holy Spirit

The Fall and Human Finiteness

The Fall of humanity has been overlooked in thinking about how we can come to know God, if at all.

- **Si integer stetisset Adam** (if Adam had not sinned) – everyone would have known God (**CALVIN'S** view).

- Knowledge of God the redeemer, mediated through Christ is part of our **REGENERATION** (of being 'born again').

- **CATHOLIC** – the Fall confused human desire for God but did not cut them off from knowledge of God completely – seen through "religious ignorance or indifference" (Catechism para. 29).

Faith

- Faith needs some **REASON** for it not to be meaningless or random.

- **CATHOLIC** – faith is not independent to reason.

- **AQUINAS** – distinguished between **formed** and **unformed** faith.

- **FORMED FAITH** - faith that wills to accept what it can believe through the intellect. Takes time and effort e.g. belief in resurrection based on witness accounts.

- **UNFORMED FAITH** - May find intellectual reasons why to believe e.g. in afterlife BUT cannot accept as truth.

- **CALVIN** – faith is firm and certain knowledge and a willingness to believe.

- **FIRM AND CERTAIN KNOWLEDGE -** Christ is direct object of faith. Firm knowledge only possible revealed through Christ and by the Holy Spirit.

- **WILLINGNESS TO BELIEVE** - an emotional and spiritual experience of assurance – given to anyone willing to accept it.

Grace

- **CATHOLIC** and **CALVINIST** teaching both agree that faith alone is not enough to know God. God's grace completes the relationship.

- **AQUINAS** – faith can only be justified by grace through the Holy Spirit.

- **CALVIN** – the Holy Spirit is a gift repairing the damage caused by Original Sin.

Revealed Knowledge Of God's Existence In Jesus Christ

Full and perfect knowledge of God is revealed in the person of Jesus Christ and through:

• The life of the **CHURCH**

• The **BIBLE**

Bible should be read from a **TRINITARIAN** perspective: God as **FATHER** (God spoke **DIRECTLY** by the **PROPHETS**); God as Christ the **MEDIATOR** (clarity and fulfilment to God's promises); **HOLY SPIRIT**

(Christians inspired).

CALVIN – Christ is mediator and mirror of God.

CATHOLIC – agrees but adds that the significance should not end with Christ but should continue with our faith, re-thinking God's revelation continuously.

Consider: can God be known by non-Christians?

The Bible And The Life Of The Church

- For traditional Catholics and Protestants, "God is the author of sacred Scripture...[and its words are] the speech of God as it is put down in writing under the breath of the Holy Spirit" (Catechism, 105).

- Christianity cannot be 'reduced' to the Bible - which is **INSPIRED** not **DICTATED** (contrast with the Qur'an - dictated by angel Gabriel).

- **CALVIN** – the Bible, read from the perspective of Jesus Christ - as revealer of God the Redeemer; prepared for in the Old Testament and culminates in the events of the New Testament.

- Bible is a significant source for knowledge of God, even for those adopting an approach of **NATURAL THEOLOGY** who might say the Bible reveals early experiences people had of God (Hebrew, as recorded in the **OLD TESTAMENT**) and to the early Christian communities.

- Knowledge of God revealed is **PERSONAL** and **COLLECTIVE**.

"In you, O Lord, I take refuge; let me never be put to shame...incline your ear to me and save me" (Psalm 71:1-2).

Q. CAN GOD BE KNOWN THROUGH REASON ALONE?

YES	NO
Natural theology – a sound and rational basis for faith. **CALVIN** - we have a sense of the divine even though it is distorted by sin and the effects of the **FALL**. Echoes St Paul in **ROMANS** - we are 'without excuse' as God's purposes are revealed in the things that are created.	**Douglas Hedley** – imagination needs to accompany reason in arguments of philosophy: "drama, prose and poetry can be considered as both creative and truthful" (Douglas Hedley: The Oxford Handbook of Natural Theology, p. 547 cited in Wilcockson & Campbell, 2016, p. 300). E.g. Plato and John's Gospel – Nicodemus' misunderstanding at being 'born again' evidences the need for imagination (John 3:1-10).
Natural theology gives an opportunity for people to share discussion about God.	**Barth** – arrogant to imagine human reason (fallible) could lead anyone into knowledge of God.
If reason is ruled out, there would be no way of testing true or false religious claims. Risk of **fideism**.	

Q. IS FAITH SUFFICIENT REASON FOR BELIEF IN GOD'S EXISTENCE?

YES	NO
Plantinga – knowledge of God can be seen as basic knowledge but only for the Christian. Not through reason but through **sensus divinitatis**.	Theological beliefs no more than wish fulfilment.
Plantinga – there can be good reasons to maintain belief, even if there cannot be incorrigible proof for it. Belief in God is no more or less rational than a lack of belief!	Theistic knowledge = irrational
Sufficient reason for belief should not depend on sense/ rational evidence alone.	**Dawkins** - faith is a cop out
Atheological objector	**Hume** – "a wise man proportions his beliefs to the evidence".

Q. IS NATURAL KNOWLEDGE OF GOD THE SAME AS REVEALED KNOWLEDGE OF GOD?

YES	NO
Things exist because God has chosen them to and in this way, God remains the source of all knowledge and has revealed everything that it is possible for us to know anything about.	**Natural knowledge** is reached through reason, while **revealed knowledge** is reached through faith.
God can reveal things to us through our reason (**Aquinas**) and this allows us to learn more about God.	Types of knowledge revealed through reason or faith are different. E.g. Trinity and life after death = revealed and not available through natural revelation.

Q. HAS THE FALL COMPLETELY REMOVED ALL NATURAL HUMAN KNOWLEDGE OF GOD?

YES	NO
Augustine – Original Sin corrupted the human will and so humans cannot approach God through their own efforts alone.	**Aquinas** – God gave us reason with purpose – to guide us in understanding our natural knowledge of God.
Barth – we cannot approach God alone; He has to approach us.	Both **natural** and **revealed** theology can be helpful.

Q. WHAT IS THE BARTH/BRUNNER DEBATE?

Brunner

- God's **general revelation** in nature allows humans to become aware of God's commands and the sinful state of humankind.

- **Jesus Christ** reveals **redemption**. Natural theology has limited purpose.

- **Imago Dei** – God's image in humans was materially but not spiritually destroyed in the Fall but not spiritually. This spiritual level allows God to address humans.

- **General revelation** – Innately sinful humans are incapable of seeing God's revelation of his nature through nature – they can know God exists but it remains a **point of contact**, no more.

- **True knowledge** – Faith in Christ is necessary for true knowledge of God.

- **Conscience** – plus guilt bring humans to awareness of God's law.

MNEMONIC: Isabella Gave Temi Cookies

Barth

- There are no points of contact in nature – human nature is absolutely corrupted by the Fall.

- Only God can choose to reveal himself to sinful humans.

Three disagreements with Brunner's interpretation of Calvin:

1. Formal self (spiritual self) cannot inform the **material**

(physical) self of God's existence. Brunner underestimates the corruption of the material self.

2. No points of contact. Nature, conscience and guilt are results of God's grace – they do not provide the points of contact themselves!

3. Order of creation. Perception of order in nature should not be basis for morality. God's moral commands are different to any natural laws. We only see order in creation after it is revealed to us through faith and the Bible.

Q. IS BELIEF IN GOD'S EXISTENCE SUFFICIENT TO PUT ONE'S TRUST IN HIM?

YES	NO
Belief rationally requires leap to **TRUST** in God.	Belief in is not the same as **TRUST** in. Trust is more personal and relational.
ANSELM - God exists necessarily, not contingently. If God is TTWNGCBC, then trust is also necessary.	Reasoned argument might not always lead to faith.
	Evil and suffering can lead to belief without trust.

Possible Exam Questions

1. Discuss critically the view that Christians can discover truths about God using human reason.

2. "Faith is all that is necessary to gain knowledge of God." Discuss.

3. "God can be known because the world is so well designed." Discuss.

4. Critically assess the view that the Bible is the only way of knowing God.

5. "Everyone has an innate knowledge of God's existence." Discuss.

6. To what extent is faith in God rational?

Key Quotes

1. "The desire for God is written in the human heart" (Catechism of the Catholic Church para. 27).

2. "No-one can look upon himself without immediately tuning his thoughts to the contemplation of God, in whom he 'lives and moves' (Acts 17:28)" (John Calvin: Institutes I.I.1).

3. "For what can be known about God is plain to them, because God has shown it to them" (Romans 1:19-20).

4. "In this ruin of mankind no one now experiences God...until Christ the Mediator comes forward to reconcile him to us". (John Calvin: Institutes I.II.1).

5. "Faith is the great cop-out, the great excuse to evade the need to think and evaluate experience" (Richard Dawkins (Edinburgh International Science Festival, April 1992) cited in Wilcockson & Campbell, 2016, p. 293).

6. "Yet even if Revelation is already complete, it has not been completely explicit; it remains for Christian faith gradually to grasp its full significance over the course of the centuries." (Catechism para. 66).

7. "The heavens are telling the glory of God; and the firmament proclaims his handiwork" (Psalm 19:1).

8. "Yet, in the first place, wherever you cast your eyes, there is no spot in the universe wherein you cannot discern at least some sparks of his glory" (John Calvin: Institutes I.V.1).

9. "Both experience and history point to a God who acts not by coercing but by evoking the response of his creatures." (Ian G. Barbour: Issues in Science and Religion (1966:463).

Person of Jesus Christ

Background & Influences

Jesus' influence as an authority comes from his teachings, his example, and his relationship with God. Jesus' moral teachings have allowed him to have authority, even for non-Christians.

As teacher of **WISDOM** (and Rabbi), Jesus developed Jewish ethics; as **LIBERATOR**, he challenged political and religious authorities; and as **SON OF GOD**, Jesus came to bring salvation and to carry out God's will on Earth.

At AS and A Level you will need to show understanding and evaluation of the different ways in which Jesus has authority: as a moral teacher of wisdom, as Son of God, and as liberator of the oppressed.

You need to show understanding and **EXEGESIS** of the following Biblical passages:

- Mark 6:47-52   **WALKING ON WATER**

- John 9:1-41   **HEALING OF THE MAN BORN BLIND**

- Matthew 5:17-48   **FULFILMENT OF THE LAW** - revised the **TORAH**

- Luke 15:11-32   **PARABLE OF LOST SON (WAITING FATHER)**

- Mark 5:24-34   **AN UNCLEAN (BLEEDING) WOMAN**

Key Terms

FORM OF LIFE - the historical, sociological, moral, and cultural conditions within which language operates. Associated with Wittgenstein.

TORAH - first five books of the Hebrew Bible (Genesis, Exodus, Leviticus, Deuteronomy and Numbers).

SERMON ON THE MOUNT - Matthew 5-7. Jesus' longest address of ethics.

METANOIA - repentance, a radical change of heart.

PARABLE OF THE LOST SON - Luke 15:11-32; deals with theme of lost and found.

ZEALOTS - 1st Century Jewish political group. Sought to overcome Roman occupation in the rebellion of 66 AD and committed mass suicide at **MASADA** (AD 74)

UNDERSIDE OF HISTORY - occupies a significant proportion of human existence but often forgotten. Sometimes refers to the oppressed or marginalised.

PREFERENTIAL OPTION FOR THE POOR - Christian duty to side with the marginalised and to act against injustice.

SAMARITANS - from Samaria. Regarded as racially and religiously impure as they had married foreigners and built their own temple.

SON OF GOD - used by followers of Jesus describing Jesus' special relationship with God.

COUNCIL OF CHALCEDON - 451 AD – re-affirm central Christian beliefs, particularly divinity and humanity of Jesus.

CHRISTOLOGY - concerned with nature of Jesus' relationship with God.

INCARNATION - 'in the flesh'.

THEOTOKOS - 'God-bearer'.

DOCETIC - Jesus only 'appeared' to be fully human so that God could communicate with humans.

EXEGESIS - close analysis and interpretation of a text.

CHRIST-EVENT - Jesus' birth, ministry, death, and resurrection.

Jesus Of History And The Christ Of Faith

1. E.P. SANDERS

- **FAITH** claims are different to claims made in the realm of reason.

- **HISTORICAL JESUS** shows a man acting within the laws of science and the limits of history. It would be a **CATEGORY MISTAKE** to venture into **HISTORY** as we would confuse history with faith.

- Jesus' teachings on hope for outcasts, non-violence and God's grace did make him significantly different to people at the time but not unique. Groups like the **ESSENES** established desert communities and taught of a coming kingdom.

2. RUDOLF BULTMANN

- The Jesus of history is less important than the **CHRIST OF FAITH.**

- The most we can know is the preaching/ teaching following Jesus' death (**KERYGMA** - the gospel of the early church).

- We should Evil and suffering can lead to belief without trust. **DEMYTHOLOGISE** the Bible (eg supposed events such as resurrection and ascension have spiritual meaning, not literal).

- The basis of Christian faith is the reflections of the early Church, inspired by their ongoing experiences of Christ; rather than the historical Jesus – of whom we can know **"almost nothing"**.

3. BLACK MESSIAH – JAMES CONE

- Starting point is **HISTORICAL** – suffering and oppression of black people

- Link to **PAUL TILLICH** – theology reflects the culture of its day and emerges from it

- Jesus is given many **TITLES** in the NT – 'Son of David', 'Good Shepherd', 'Son of God'. 'Black Messiah' continues this tradition. Jesus would not have been white. Metaphor - Jesus' suffering in unity with the oppressed.

- **CROSS** – not just a symbol, it resonates with the **'lynching tree'**. Both Jesus and blacks died and suffered – on a cross – as a result of injustice.

Jesus Christ's Authority As Son Of God

Expressed In his Knowledge of God, Miracles and Resurrection

1. Son of God and Messiah (Mark 6:47-52; John 9:1-41)

In Jewish terms, often used to refer to the King, anointed by God to do His will on Earth. Hoped that an anointed person would deliver Israel politically, morally and spiritually.

• Hebrew for anointed – **MESSIAH**

• Greek for anointed – **CHRISTOS**

• Son of God = **CHRIST**(os)

"Truly this man was God's Son!" (Mark 15:39) – remarked by Roman Centurion at Jesus' death. It is unclear whether the centurion meant Jesus was **the** Son of God or **a** son of God.

Christian leaders accepted Jesus as both fully God and fully human.

2. Christology from Above

• Focus is on Jesus' **DIVINITY** and God's act of bringing humanity back into relationship with him.

• Known as **HIGH CHRISTOLOGY**.

• Relies on faith, cannot be proved.

3. Christology from Below

- Focus is on Jesus' **MESSAGE**, teaching and the example he sets.

- The focus of salvation is on how people **RESPOND** to Jesus and the way this helps to develop their relationship to God and the world.

- Known as **LOW CHRISTOLOGY**.

4. Did Jesus Think He Was Son of God?

- If Jesus thought he was fully human – how can we claim he knew he was God's Son?

- In **Exodus**, God reveals his identity as "I am who I am" (Exodus 3:14).

- **John's Gospel** - Jesus uses similar statements - "I am the way, and the truth, and the life. No one comes to the Father except through me" (John 14:6).

- **"The Father is greater than I" (John14:28)**. Does this imply that Jesus saw himself as limited by his own humanity?

5. Miracles do not necessarily indicate Jesus' Divinity

- Miracles - special insights into Jesus' teaching on the nature of God's **KINGDOM**.

- No single word for 'miracle' in New Testament. They might not point to the laws of nature being broken. Instead, 'mighty works', 'signs' and 'wonders' indicate something deeper about the nature of God and reality.

- **LOW CHRISTOLOGY** – Jesus' miracles understood like parables of **CREATION** (such as stilling the storm) or **REDEMPTION** (such as raising the paralysed man with the words 'your sins are forgiven", Mark 2)

6. Birth and Incarnation

- **Luke 1:35** – Jesus born of a Virgin, Mary.

- **Chalcedonian Definition** – Mary conceives God in human form – incarnation.

- Mary – **THEOTOKOS** (God-bearer).The Council of Ephesus decreed in 431 that Mary is the Theotokos because her son Jesus is both God and man: one divine person with two natures (divine and human) intimately and **HYPOSTATICALLY** united (humanity and divinity in one hypostasis, or individual existence).

Some Heretical Views

NESTORIUS (d.c.451) – Christ's divine and human natures were completely separate. Humanity and divinity come together as one when Jesus' will becomes one with God's will.

APOLLINARIUS (c.310-390) – Incarnation meant that God's will replaced Jesus' human reason. Jesus was a complete person and experienced suffering, still had a soul but could not sin as he would have no 'inner conflict'.

DOCETIC CHRISTIANS – Incarnation involved God only appearing to assume human flesh. Jesus could not have been fully human as he was fully God, bringing salvation through this knowledge.

Miracles As Signs Of Salvation

1. Redemption and Creation Miracles

Agreed by both **HIGH** and **LOW** Christologies.

Echoes **Isaiah's** vision of a renewed society with new insight.

• E.g. **healing of man born blind** (John 9:1-41) focuses more on the man's awareness of Jesus as saviour, than on the process of the man's sight being saved. **REDEMPTION MIRACLE.**

• **Jesus' walking on water** (Mark 6:47-52) indicates how salvation applies to the whole of the universe; reminiscent of God's spirit hovering over the chaotic water at the point of Creation (Genesis 1:2). **CREATION MIRACLE.**

2. Resurrection as Miracle

A Jewish idea taught by **PHARISEES** that the righteous would be raised to live in God's Kingdom at the end of time.

Jesus' resurrection was different – witnessed by many over a long period; marked the beginning of a **NEW ERA** as early followers experienced a change in their relationship with God.

St PAUL – everything can be brought into completion by God. The resurrection was the '**FIRST FRUITS**' (**1 CORINTHIANS 15:20**)

WOLFHART PANNENBURG – Jesus was an ordinary human in his lifetime but the resurrection was a decisive moment in history, a unique sign of God's accomplishment of creation at the end of days, revealing Jesus as God's Son.

3. Doubting Thomas

- "Then he said to Thomas, 'Put your finger here and see my hands. Reach out your hand and put it in my side. Do not doubt but believe.' Thomas answered him, 'My Lord and my God!'". (John 20:27-28).

- Jesus' body is not just transformed spiritually but also allows the experience of the presence of God.

- A **RELIGIOUS EXPERIENCE** – Jesus' resurrection allows him to be witnessed to and worshipped as God without being blasphemous.

- Those who believe 'without seeing' are commended. (John 20)

- The resurrection gives authority to proclaim Jesus as God's Son.

Jesus As Moral Teacher

Jesus' moral teaching on repentance and forgiveness, inner purity and moral motivation (MATTHEW 5:17-48; LUKE 15:11-32)

1. The Living Word (John 1)

WITTGENSTEIN - Jesus' authority is derived from him as a teacher of wisdom. He affirmed **AUTHENTIC LIVING.**

Jesus embodied the **MORAL** and **SPIRITUAL** and so was the **LIVING WORD** ('The word became flesh and lived among us', John 1)

2. Jesus' Moral Teaching

- Jesus uses **PARABLES**, short sayings, actions, examples and healings to express moral message.

- Jesus as the **NEW MOSES** founding a **NEW ISRAEL** (argument of theologian **TOM WRIGHT**).

- "Do not think that I have come to abolish the Law or the Prophets; I have not come to abolish them but to **FULFIL** them." (Matthew 5:17).

3. Forgiveness and Repentance

- **METANOIA** (repentance or radical change of heart) – At the heart of Jesus' teaching on the arrival of the Kingdom of God.

- Examples include **ZACCHAEUS** (tax collector) and the **PARABLE OF THE PRODIGAL SON** (

- Forgiveness brings about mental (end of guilt) and material freedom(forgive our debts).

- Seen in Lord's Prayer.

4. Personal Responsibility

- Keeping the Sabbath holy is an important religious law **(Ten Commandments, Exodus 20:1-17).**

- It is also an important social law as it is a **foundation for social justice** – everyone is entitled to one day free from work during the week.

- Jesus argued people misused Sabbath rules in order to avoid social responsibility. Rabbis had developed 39 different definitions and examples of work (which had to be avoided). Jesus argued that **in focusing on this religious duty, people were avoiding their duty to humanity.**

- "The Sabbath was made for humankind, not humankind for the Sabbath" (Jesus, Mark 2:27).

- Despite the risk of death penalty for breaking the Sabbath rules, Jesus broke these to heal the sick and allowed his disciples to 'pick corn' to eat.

- Morality is not 'blind obedience'. It requires personal responsibility and **PURITY** of mind.

- Religious practices should serve human **NEEDS**.

Jesus As Liberator

Jesus' role as liberator of the marginalised, his challenge to political & religious authority (MARK 5:24-34; LUKE 10:25-37).

Some Key Authors

1. S.G.F.BRANDON JESUS AND THE ZEALOTS (1967) - later writers made Jesus out to be a pacifist, toning down the reality that he was in fact a politically-driven activist – a freedom fighter.

• Preferential Option for the Poor

• The Underside of History

Jesus shows a bias to these groups, despite the Church presenting him as politically neutral, a spiritual teacher.

2. GUSTAVO GUTIÉRREZ MERINO (1928-) A THEOLOGY OF LIBERATION

• Father of **LIBERATION THEOLOGY.**

• Seeing Jesus as liberator makes him (the Christ of faith) 'really engaged' in the world and allows us to see the people of the Bible as more than just fictitious characters.

• Jesus' historical example as **PREFERENTIAL OPTION FOR THE POOR** sets the expectation for modern Christians.

• Jesus more than a **ZEALOT** - did not set himself up as a national leader - encouraged his followers not to think of him in that way. Jesus' mission was also not only to save Israel but **ALL** human societies.

3. CAMILLO TORRES RESTREPO (1929-66): ROMAN CATHOLIC PRIEST

- Joined communist guerrilla group (National Libertarian Army of Columbia) in their active resistance against the government.

- No longer a priest by the time of fighting but still thought of his actions in a priestly way.

Liberator of the Marginalised

Many parables deal with help of the outcast – often, sinners (**HAMARTALOI**). These include the 'unclean' (diseased, paralysed), tax collectors, sexually impure, religious heretics and the uneducated (fishermen, labourers).

Jesus - **MORAL MESSAGE** - often delivered through the example of those considered impure rather than the religious leaders.

- Luke 10:25-37 (Good Samaritan)

- Mark 5:24-34 (contrast with Leviticus 15:19-28) Bleeding Woman

- "The last shall be first, and the first last" (Matthew 20:16).

Jesus rejected table-fellowship **RITUALS** of the Pharisees (ritual washing, food laws etc.) Indicates his vision of the Kingdom of God as a transformed society.

Q. WAS JESUS ONLY A TEACHER OF WISDOM?

YES	NO
Bultmann and Hick - we need to strip away the impossible – miracles, demons etc. Once we do this, we are left with an authentic Jesus, teacher of wisdom.	Jesus' wisdom stretched beyond morality and to spiritual concerns of forgiveness and salvation.
Jesus as 'teacher of wisdom' is appealing to those who find his divinity hard to accept.	Resurrection is crucial to understanding Jesus' message. Impact of Jesus goes beyond rationality.
What would set him apart from other teachers of wisdom?	Resurrection was a unique event and different from contemporary understandings of resurrection.

Q. IS JESUS MORE THAN A LIBERATOR?

YES	NO
Some see Jesus' leadership as **SPIRITUAL**, not just political – see reply to Pilate during trial.	Jesus asks not to be called Messiah or King (e.g. **John 6:15**).
Evidence suggests Jesus did not advocate **VIOLENCE** in revolution: "Put your sword back in its place," Jesus said to **PETER**, "for all who draw the sword will die by the sword." (**Matthew 26:52**)	Even Jesus' spiritual side can be seen as **LIBERATION** – from sin and from death. Makes him more than a figure of history but still a liberator, even if spiritual.

Q. WAS JESUS' RELATIONSHIP WITH GOD VERY SPECIAL OR TRULY UNIQUE?

VERY SPECIAL	TRULY UNIQUE
Sanders: uniqueness cannot be verified through historical claims. Resurrection doesn't count as cannot be analysed historically.	**Christ-Event**: Everyone lives their own historical existence in a different way and in that sense, everyone is unique. Jesus is no different in that respect.
John Macquarrie – question of uniqueness is ambiguous and should be left alone. Jesus' life is **a** defining moment in human relationship God; but not exclusive.	**Resurrection** uniquely reveals Christ's divinity.
Jesus Seminar – many of Jesus' sayings are not his and those that are authentic do not reveal a uniquely different person.	Jesus Offers 'the Way' not 'a Way' to a new relationship with God. **John 14**: - "I am the way, and the truth, and the life".
Theologians almost remove any 'uniqueness' when they try to present Jesus as a universal, timeless figure. Jesus becomes of 'general interest' and indistinct.	**New Testament Letters and Acts** mark Jesus' relationship with God as unique.

Q. DID JESUS THINK HE WAS DIVINE?

YES	NO
Talks about death and sin with authority.	Jesus' doubts e.g. Gethsemane. Human emotions allowed him to have a life comparable with ours.
Teaching on God's love and forgiveness.	Self-knowledge is extremely complex — even for modern-day humans!
How could he have been fully human if his miracles, power & authority were true?	**William Wrede** argued Jesus' Messianic claims were an invention of the early church - in Mark Jesus rebukes anyone who suggested he was the Messiah.

Possible Exam Questions

1. "There is no evidence to suggest that Jesus thought of himself as divine." Discuss.

2. To what extent can Jesus be regarded as no more than a teacher of wisdom?

3. "Jesus' role was just to liberate the poor and weak against oppression." Discuss.

4. Assess the view that the miracles prove Jesus was the Son of God.

5. "Jesus Christ is not unique." Discuss.

6. To what extent was Jesus just a teacher of morality?

Key Quotes

1. "The use of such words as 'unique' and 'unprecedented' shows that [scholars] have shifted their perspective from that of critical history and exegesis to that of faith." (E.P. Sanders, Jesus and Judaism, p. 320).

2. "Christ's blackness is both literal and symbolic. His blackness is literal in the sense that he truly becomes One with the oppressed blacks, taking their suffering as his suffering and revealing that he is found in the history of our struggle, the story of our pain." (J. Cone, God of the Oppressed, p. 136).

3. "The Father and I are one" (John 10:30).

4. "Whoever has seen me has seen the Father" (John 14:9).

5. "Jesus accompanies his words with many 'mighty works and wonders and signs' which manifest that the kingdom is present in him and attest that he was the promised Messiah." (Catechism of the Catholic Church para. 547).

6. "So miracles strengthen faith in the One who does his Father's works; they bear witness that he is the Son of God" (Catechism of the Catholic Church para. 548).

7. "Only because the end of the world is already present in Jesus' resurrection is God revealed in him" (W. Pannenberg, Jesus – God and Man, 1968, p. 69).

8. "Jesus said, "My kingdom is not of this world. If it were, my servants would fight to prevent my arrest by the Jewish leaders. But now my kingdom is from another place." (John 18:36).

9. "The duty of every Catholic is to be a revolutionary. The duty of every revolutionary is to make the revolution" (Restrepo, speech, 1965, cited in Wilcockson, Wilkinson, & Campbell, 2016, p. 311).

10. "If Jesus were alive today, He would be a guerrillero" (Restrepo, cited in Wilcockson, Wilkinson, & Campbell, 2016, p. 311).

Christian Moral Principles

Diversity of Christian Moral Reasoning, Practices & Sources of Ethics

Background And Influences

"All Scripture is inspired by God, and is useful for teaching, for reproof, for correction, for training in righteousness" (2 Timothy 3:16).

The following questions are relevant:

1. If the Bible does reveal God's will and if it is true that only Biblical ethical commands must be followed; then what can be helpful in discerning how to follow scripture?

2. If God is the author of the Bible, does this mean that it, alone, must be used for moral instruction?

3. If the Bible is **INFALLIBLE,** and we cannot understand it, is the problem with the reader rather than with the text?

At AS and A Level, you will need to show understanding and evaluation of the Bible as the only authority for Christian ethical practices; Bible, Church and reason as the sources of Christian ethical practices; and love (**AGAPE**) as the only Christian ethical principle which governs Christian practices.

Key Terms

AGAPE - Greek for 'love'. Also, refers to Jesus' sacrificial and generous love for others

AUTONOMOUS CHRISTIAN ETHICS - ethics are self-governed.

BIBLE/ SCRIPTURE - collection of books in the Bible which contain God's revelation.

BIBLICISM - belief that the Bible is the revealed word of God and that God directly inspired the writers of the Bible.

COVENANT - God's special promises and agreement made with humans which requires special behaviour from them.

CHURCH TRADITION - traditions of how Christian life in community works in worship, practical moral life, and prayer. The teaching and reflection of the Church handed down across time.

HETERONOMOUS CHRISTIAN ETHICS - several sources of authority or law govern ethics (eg Natural Law, Bible, Reason).

HERMENEUTICAL - study of the principles of interpreting the Bible

INTRINSIC - in itself/ essential.

MAGISTERIUM - the official teaching of the Church entrusted to the Pope and his bishops (eg contained in the **CATECHISM** and **ENCYCLICALS**)

PAPAL ENCYCLICAL - letter issued by the Pope to his senior clergy on some significant topic or teaching; has doctrinal authority.

PRIMA SCRIPTURA - the Bible is the principle source of authority but is understood through and with Church teaching and reason.

SACRED TRADITION - the revelation of Jesus Christ is communicated in two ways: through Scripture, and through the apostolic and authoritative teaching of the Church councils and the Pope.

SOLA SCRIPTURA - exclusive following of the Bible.

THEONOMOUS CHRISTIAN ETHICS - God's law or commands govern ethics. Living the good life must be revealed by God, since we are by nature, sinful.

Different Approaches To A Christian Moral Reading Of The Bible

Hermeneutic Factors

Richard B. Hays proposes many factors to consider when thinking about how Christians use the Bible to help them to make moral decisions.

1. **Accuracy** different gospels relate slightly different versions

2. **Range** of issues may be limited by cultural context

3. **Frequency** of use of sections

4. **Management** of different texts

5. **Focal images** metaphors can be interpreted different ways

MNEMONIC: Angus Ran For Max's Football

HAYS also proposed questions of interpretation (**HERMENEUTICS**):

1. Is there a focus on **symbolism**?

2. Is there a focus on **rules**?

3. Is there a focus on **principles**?

4. Is there a focus on **paradigms**?

MNEMONIC: Sophie Really Painted Poppies

Propositional & Non-propositional Revelation

PROPOSITIONAL KNOWLEDGE - knowing or accepting something as true e.g. knowing the date of your birthday. Has a truth value – can be true, false, or somewhere in the middle.

PROPOSITIONAL REVELATION - knowledge revealed by God, not through reason. E.g. God's moral standards.

PROPOSITIONAL APPROACH TO THE BIBLE - the words in the Bible are messages from God. There are fixed moral messages and meanings e.g. in parables and Sermon on the Mount.

NON-PROPOSITIONAL KNOWLEDGE - other kinds of knowledge e.g. how to do something.

NON-PROPOSITIONAL REVELATION - belief or faith in God through personal encounter or experience.

NON-PROPOSITIONAL APPROACH TO THE BIBLE - God's

revelation in Jesus was through Jesus' human life, not through a book. The Bible acts as a doorway into meeting the living God.

The Bible as Sole Authority for Ethics

If the Bible reveals God's will, then only Bible commands must be followed

1. Ethics can be shown in the Bible as **THEONOMOUS**.

2. Ethics can be expressed through **COVENANT** (a legal agreement).

THEONOMOUS ethics are shown through real life situations, rather than as clear commandments.

E.g. **King David's** adultery with Bathsheba (**2 Samuel 11**) illustrates what living 'the moral life' is NOT. David is not just judged on his adherence to the commandments but on the type of person he became. Uriah (Bathsheba's husband who was killed in battle) strikes a complete contrast.

Must be understood in the theological context of life lived as a **COVENANT** agreement with mutual obligations, with God.

The **OLD TESTAMENT** establishes ethics as both **SOCIAL** and **PERSONAL**. The **TEN COMMANDMENTS** are evidence of this (**Exodus 20:1-17**). Other Biblical examples:

- **Amos and Isaiah** – Old Testament Prophets – focus on social justice and see a proper response to God's covenant to be **treatment of the poor**.

- **New Testament**: Jesus' **Sermon on the Mount** (Matthew 5-7) –

the new covenant is not just about following the laws set out in the Old Testament but involves the inner laws of love, peace, faith, and righteousness – **"be perfect as your heavenly Father is perfect" (Matthew 5:48).**

- Modelled on Jesus' sacrifice, **St Paul** uses '**living sacrifice**' (Romans 12:1) to describe Christian covenantal life. This makes devotion to God and love of neighbour above anything else.

Literalism - Is It Realistic?

- "If your right eye causes you to sin, tear it out and throw it away" (Matthew 5:29).

- **KARL BARTH** – scripture has high value but literalism could be dangerous as it gives the bible a divine status that can only rightly be given to God. This is **BIBLIOLATRY** – false worship of the Bible.

- Words of the bible are a **WITNESS** to God's Word revealed through the different writers of the Bible over time. It is not the 'Word' itself.

- Bible must be read **CRITICALLY** as a source of inspiration. It is not truth itself, despite being a source of moral truth.

- **HUMAN REASON** must be taken into account.

Contradictions

1. Old Testament

- War and **RETRIBUTIVE JUSTICE**: "an eye for an eye, a tooth for a tooth" (**Exodus 21:24**).

- Capital punishment apparent for **BLASPHEMY** (**Genesis 9:6**).

- Capital punishment for those who undermine social and divine order, adultery (**Deuteronomy 22:22**); dishonouring parents (**Numbers 1:51**), homosexual acts (**Leviticus 18**).

- **Deuteronomy 20:10-20** – sets out rules of war, Israelites allowed to kill foreign women and children of the coastal tribes.

2. New Testament

- Sermon on the Mount (**Matthew 5-7**) – consciously revises old law in **LEVITICUS** (eg 'eye for an eye' becomes 'turn the other cheek')

- **RECONCILIATION** replaces retribution (**Matthew 5:38-42**) and love of enemies is taught in addition (**Matthew 5:44**).

- Jesus stressing a future ideal – **KINGDOM OF GOD**, similar to how previous prophets in the Old testament had ventured (**Micah 4:1-4**).

- Meanwhile, in an imperfect world, violence might be a **NECESSARY EVIL** (Augustine, Luther).

- Others argue Biblical **PACIFISM** (Martin Luther King Jr) is a Christian duty as it lay at heart of Jesus' teaching on love.

Strengths Of Bible - Sole Authority

1. Makes the Bible **INFALLIBLE** (unchallengeable) and **INERRANT** (no mistakes).

2. Can be trusted and relied upon **AS INSPIRED BY GOD** (2 Timothy 3:16).

3. **RICHARD MOUW** – "just because there is one biblical commandment, a law of love, does not rule out the possibility of other biblical commandments on other matters" (Summarised and cited in Ahluwalia & Bowie, 2016, p. 392).

4. Seeing the Bible as infallible can provide a helpful framework for living – decisions about **TAKING LIFE** (Sermon on Mount); attitudes towards **SEXUALITY** (Old Testament, St Paul); attitudes towards **MARRIAGE** (Genesis and Jesus' teachings).

Weaknesses Of Bible As Sole Authority

1. We can't separate ourselves from our own reading of the text – impossible not to read **subjectively** and with **interpretation**.

2. If God dictated, then why so many **different styles** e.g. John's Gospel is much more mystical and theological.

3. **Conflicts** arise – Jesus' attitude to Jewish laws eg Leviticus and the bleeding woman of Mark 5 (no longer unclean, as Jesus accepts her).

4. Many Christians do not follow all the 'rules' in the Bible and some do not even appear to refer to moral living e.g. **Leviticus 19:27** – limits

the cutting of facial and head hair; **Leviticus 19:19** bans planting two crops in the same field.

Bible Church & Reason

Christian Ethics must involve a combination of Biblical teaching, Church teaching and human reason

Christian ethics should combine Biblical and Church teaching with human **REASON** to account for new situations.

- **PRIMA SCRIPTURA** – the Bible is the principle source of authority but is understood through and with Church teaching and reason.

- **RICHARD HAYS** and **WILLIAM SPOHN** – you cannot study scripture without reference to the Church communities and traditions in which it operates. **SPOHN** suggests three interconnecting pillars: 1. the New Testament story of Jesus; 2. the ethics of virtue and character; and 3. the practices of Christian spirituality.

Ethical Heteronomy - Roman Catholicism

- Christian ethics are can be accessed through the **natural world, Church authority, reason,** and **conscience**. Together, these make up the **NATURAL LAW**.

- Biblical grounding – **Romans 2:15** – even Gentiles (non-Jews) can behave morally when acting according to their conscience and 'the law of God written on their hearts'.

Thomas Aquinas' Natural Law

- Humans are set apart from other animals because of our ability to use human reason to know God's **ETERNAL LAW**.

- Human experience of God's eternal law is based on **SELF-EVIDENT** principle – do good, avoid evil - **SYNDERESIS**. Goodness is the goal of human flourishing.

Magisterium - Roman Catholic

- **COLLECTIVE WISDOM** of Church leaders and teachers, published in **PAPAL ENCYCLICALS** (circulated letters).

- In all ordinary circumstances, the **MAGISTERIUM** should be followed – it has authority.

- "The Church, the 'pillar and **BULWARK** of the truth', 'has received this solemn command of Christ from the apostles to announce the saving truth'." (Catechism of the Catholic Church, 2032).

Veritatis Splendor (Splendour of Truth)

- 1996, Pope John Paul II – **VERITATIS SPLENDOR** – **ENCYCLICAL** reasserts centrality of reason, conscience, natural law, and Magisterium in moral theology.

- Moral law = knowable to all through **REASON, NATURAL LAW** and **CONSCIENCE**.

- Humans are **SINFUL** and cannot rely on reason alone. Church acts as a guide.

- Some moral acts are **INTRINSICALLY** wrong. It is never right to contradict the moral order.

Liberation Theology

- 1960s onwards - popular in **LATIN AMERICA**.

- Bible = centre of ethics.

- **ETHICS FROM BELOW**– begins with the marginalised, **ENGAGES** with political and economic struggles against the **POWERS**; suspicious of 'top-down' traditional Church teaching.

- Some use of **MARXISM**, but criticised, as while it is good at questioning power, it also criticises religion for being exploitative and an **OPIUM OF THE PEOPLE** reinforcing false consciousness (acceptance) of their oppression.

Conscience & Tradition

- Protestant Natural Law theologians – **Richard Hooker (1554-1600); Hugo Grotius (1583-1645).** Bible evolved over time, developing out of the needs of communities and therefore reason and conscience should guide its use in ethics (like Catholicism but no magisterium).

Stanley Hauerwas

- Christian ethics can only be done in the **Christian worshipping community**.

- Jesus adapted Old Testament teaching in his **Sermon on the Mount** and we continue to **adapt tradition** today.

- Jesus' sermon was aimed at Christian community, not leaders. It includes examples of Christian values that must be developed in communities, in response to God, **siding with the marginalised.**

- Christian communities need to question society's values by living and practising Christian **SOCIAL VIRTUES** (loyalty, trust, faithfulness, forgiveness, reconciliation).

Q. DIFFERENCES IN CATHOLIC AND PROTESTANT VIEWS OF HOW BIBLE, CHURCH, AND REASON WORK IN MORAL QUESTIONS

CATHOLIC	PROTESTANT
Relying on sacred tradition is trust in the **CHURCH'S AUTHORITY**.	Some recognise Church tradition but acknowledge that this might **CHANGE WITH TIME.**
Church teachings on moral questions are to be **TRUSTED** like the Bible and obeyed but not without thinking – this allows conscience to play a role.	In **EVANGELICAL CHRISTIANITY** only the Bible is **INFALLIBLE** and **INERRANT**.
REASON provides another direct source of revelation e.g. through nature and the moral laws implicit in this created world.	Reason can provide a way of **INTERPRETING** and making sense of the Bible.
There is **ONE SOURCE** of revelation but the Bible, reason, and Church tradition provide different ways of **accessing** this.	Emphasis on **PREACHING** the word, but critical methods eg source comparisons used - compare stories in different gospels

Criticisms Of The Bible, Faith & Reason

1. Problem of <u>Sources</u>: What are legitimate sources for Christian ethics? Are some sources e.g. Marxism, alien to Christian thinking? Do some sources have greater authority than others? If so, what principles determine the hierarchy of these sources?

2. <u>Deviation</u> from Bible: some accuse Catholic tradition of breaking away from the Bible e.g. **Martin Luther**, German Reformer.

3. Jesus' attitude to <u>Tradition</u>: Jesus appears to criticise religious traditions e.g. Pharisees' focus on ritual cleanliness.

4. <u>Law</u> of love: should prevail over traditions (**Rudolf Bultmann**).

5. Justice, love, and wisdom: three ethical norms that should work together for Christians (**Paul Tillich**), the most important of which is love and not the following of fixed rules that influence '**moral Puritanism**' – the groups that aligns the Christian message with fixed rules about foods, drinks, and sexual relations.

MNEMONIC: Sort David's Traditional Lovely Pie

Agape Love Is All

Jesus' only command was to love and human reason must decide how to apply this (Fletcher's Situation Ethics)

Autonomous

- Love should be the only governing Christian principle – summarised in

Jesus' own sacrificial life

- **Hans Küng**: supports **autonomy**.

- There is nothing in Christian ethics that could not be found in any person with good will.

- **Pope Francis** encourages moral guidance rooted in love. The rules of Catholic tradition should be recognised but so should modern challenges of human relationships.

Applied to Euthanasia

- Contrary to official Catholic moral teaching but not the principles of Catholic reasoning and conscience to keep someone alive at all costs.

- Jesus specifically challenged rule-based ethics and encouraged autonomy. **Mark 7:14-23** - Jesus declares all foods **CLEAN** in opposition to Levitical purity code..

- We should not ask if euthanasia is right or wrong but rather, does it respect a person's life?

- Rejected by 'faith-ethic' Catholic theologians for undermining Magisterium e.g. **Joseph Ratzinger (Pope Benedict XVI).**

Q. ARE CHRISTIAN ETHICS DISTINCTIVE?

YES	NO
Deontological - DUTY BASED	Relative - to a certain culture and time - so Christian values change
Bible is a **distinctive** text	Some take a more **pragmatic** and freer approach to ethical decision-making.
Christian ethics will sometimes differ from the values of society – they **ARE** distinctive	Joseph Fletcher argues in **SITUATION ETHICS** that agape makes Christian ethics relativistic and pragmatic
Set apart from ethics that start with **human desire** e.g. Utilitarianism	Christians seem **INVISIBLE** eg materialistic, Capitalist, warmongering and anti-women
Set apart from ethics that use **reason** and moral law but do not need the Bible e.g. Kantian ethics and Natural Moral Law.	Jesus had one robe, no house, preached peace, and asked the rich young man to give up everything for the Kingdom; but modern Christians don't

Q. IS THE PRINCIPLE OF LOVE SUFFICIENT?

YES	NO
Joseph Fletcher and **James Gustafson** - Goodness is a condition of being human. **Fletcher** – Situation Ethics – every situation should be judged relatively to the principle of love and guided by four **'working principles'**: **PRAGMATISM, RELATIVISM, POSITIVISM, PERSONALISM.**	There is more to Jesus' teaching than love. E.g. Jesus' **Sermon on the Mount** did not completely lose law, but sought to 'fulfil' it **(Matthew 5:17)** by considering how to develop it inwardly in relationship with God in overcoming sin.
Appealing for Christians living in a secular western culture	Christian values need to be grounded in the Christian **NARRATIVE** dealing with the likes of forgiveness, human nature, redemption, afterlife, and community. Belief in these **DOES** make a difference to the values and moral actions of a person
GOOD SAMARITAN (LUKE 10) is a key story of a situationist approach 'go and do likewise', says Jesus	**Tillich** – it is not just love – it needs defining as love with a foundation of justice and outcome of forgiveness and compassion too.
Jesus refuses to condemn the adulterous woman **(JOHN 8)**	What about the other commands of the Bible? **(MOUW)**

Q. IS THE BIBLE A COMPREHENSIVE MORAL GUIDE?

YES	NO
Contains poems, histories, narratives, letters, laws.	Rooted in a **particular cultural community** in a small corner of the Middle East.
Many examples of how different people have responded to moral dilemmas and how God has spoken to them throughout.	Shows how a particular culture responded to universal moral situations – how can this be **generalised**?
Bible is God's Word, revelation of the living God who created all. It **can provide a voice for many situations.**	Bible **reflects limitations of their time** and culture e.g. attitudes toward women, abortion, homosexuality
Contains broad principles based on God's character of **LOVE**, justice, faithfulness, forgiveness, mercy and sacrifice.	Has not benefitted from **modern knowledge** and nor does it contain guidance on modern-day moral dilemmas e.g. aspects of genetic modification.

Q. ARE CHRISTIAN ETHICS PERSONAL OR COMMUNAL?

PERSONAL	COMMUNAL
Jesus had arguments within his community and acted as an **'individual'** with his willingness to break rules and question the Pharisees.	Can't study scripture without referring to the communities and traditions from which it came and in which it operates.
Jesus sets an **example** for Christians as individuals.	An individual Christian belongs to the **community of faith** and this has a claim over the individual.
Example set by Jesus is not **prescriptive** or **legalistic**, but rooted in love.	Bible is for the people of God collectively, not the individual. OT = **COVENANT**, NT = **KINGDOM**

Possible Exam Questions

1. How fair is the claim that there is nothing distinctive about Christian ethics?

2. "The Bible is all that is needed as a moral guide for Christian behaviour." Discuss.

3. "The Church should decide what is morally good." Discuss.

4. Assess the view that the Bible is a comprehensive moral guide for Christians.

5. To what extent do Christians actually disagree about what Christian ethics are?

6. "Christian moral principles are not self-evident." Discuss.

Key Quotes

1. "Prophecy never had its origin in the human will, but prophets, though human, spoke from God as they were carried along by the Holy Spirit". 2 Peter 1:20-21.

2. "Then the Lord reached out his hand and touched my mouth and said to me, 'I have put my words in your mouth.'" Jeremiah 1:9.

3. "Just because there is one biblical commandment, a law of love, does not rule out the possibility of other biblical commandments on other matters" (Richad Mouw, surmised and cited in Ahluwalia & Bowie, 2016, p. 392).

4. "The interpretation of Scripture can never occur in a vacuum". (Richard Hays, The Moral Vision of the New Testament, 1996, p. 209).

5. "Sacred tradition and Sacred Scripture form one sacred deposit of the word of God, committed to the Church". (Vatican II Council, Dei Verbum, 'Dogmatic Constitution on Divine Revelation,' par. 10. In Vatican Council II: The Conciliar Documents, ed. Flannery, 1975.

6. "This teaching office [magisterium] is not above the Word of God, but serves it". (Vatican II Council, Dei Verbum, 'Dogmatic Constitution on Divine Revelation,' par. 10. In Vatican Council II: The Conciliar Documents, ed. Flannery, 1975.

7. "The Church, the 'pillar and bulwark of the truth', 'has received this solemn command of Christ from the apostles to announce the saving truth'." Catechism of the Catholic Church para. 2032.

8. "This is my commandment, that you love one another as I have loved you. No one has greater love than this, to lay down one's life for one's friends" (John 15:12-13).

9. "Love does not delight in evil but rejoices with the truth. [7] It always protects, always trusts, always hopes, always perseveres." St Paul (1 Corinthians 13:6-7).

10. "All Scripture is inspired by God and profitable for teaching, for rebuke and for training in righteousness". (1 Timothy, 3:16)

Christian Moral Action

Background & Influences

- **BONHOEFFER'S ETHICS** - Our sinful nature means that no human decision can ever be absolutely right or wrong. Sometimes, we can act only **out of despair but in faith and hope.** It is impossible to accurately predict all possible outcomes of an action. Consequentialist approaches to moral action are rejected.

- **MARTIN LUTHER** - State ruling brought order to the natural sinful inclination of humans towards disorder. Bonhoeffer was different and emphasised the **AUTHORITY** of God over that of the state.

At AS an A Level, you will need to explain and evaluate the teaching and example of Dietrich Bonhoeffer on **DUTY** to God and **DUTY** to the State, the Church as community and source of spiritual discipline, and the cost of discipleship.

Key Terms

CHEAP GRACE - grace that is offered freely, but is received without any change in the person.

CONSEQUENTIAL ETHICS - any form of ethics which judges the rightness or wrongness of an act by its outcomes.

COSTLY GRACE - grace followed by obedience to God's command and discipleship.

DISCIPLESHIP - following the life, teaching, and example of Jesus.

LIBERAL SOCIETIES - societies which develop their laws based on the principle that humans flourish when given maximum freedoms and minimum control by governments.

NO RUSTY SWORDS - Bonhoeffer's metaphor to describe the outworn ethical attitudes which the Church has used and have no use today.

PASSION - Jesus' sufferings at the end of his life.

RELIGIONLESS CHRISTIANITY - Bonhoeffer's description of Christianity without the baggage of the past and contamination by the ideological beliefs of the present.

SECULAR PACIFISM - secular means 'of this world'. Pacifism - violence and war are wrong. Bonhoeffer invented the term 'secular pacifism' to show a false non-religious belief that society can achieve a state of non-violence.

SOLIDARITY - an selfless commitment to stand alongside, and be with those less fortunate.

THE WESTERN VOID - Bonhoeffer's description of the state of the Western secular world without Christianity filled with all kinds of dangerous beliefs and ideas.

TYRANNICIDE - the deliberate killing of tyrant for the common good.

UTOPIA - refers to an ideal state where everything is perfect.

WORLD COME OF AGE - used by Bonhoeffer to describe how the

Western culture has grown up and in embracing a rational view of the world has discarded a superstitious view of religion.

Duty To God & To The State

Bonhoeffer's teaching on the duty to Church and State

Responsibility to the State

Christians have a **RESPONSIBILITY** to the state. They must work to ensure the state acts in accordance to **GOD'S WILL**.

Sometimes, the state gains too much power and **JUSTICE** is set below policy. Other times, the state assumes it is 'justice itself' and uses this to justify any action. The state fails to acknowledge its **OBEDIENCE TO THE WILL OF GOD**.

BONHOEFFER – the state can NEVER represent the will of God and therefore, the state can NEVER adopt ultimate power.

The Church is to keep the state in check – not be a part of it.

Obedience, Leadership & Doing God's Will

Christians have a duty to **DISOBEY** if the state is making reasonable people face difficult situations.

The Church was being fooled into believing **NAZISM** was bringing order to a disordered society.

"Hitler is the way of the Spirit and the will of God for the German people to enter the church of Christ" (Hermann Gruner, quoted in Geffrey B. Kelly et al., Dietrich Bonhoeffer: The Life of a Modern Martyr (Christianity Today Essentials), 2012

The ostracism of minorities and disrespect for life was a disregard for **GOD-GIVEN ORDER**.

Establishing social order may justify **TYRANNICIDE** as a Christian duty.

A Christian can only act in faith and in hope – influenced by **MARTIN LUTHER** - **'here I stand, I can do no other'**.

LUTHERAN TEACHING – God ordained two kingdoms:

1. The **spiritual kingdom** of Christ, governed by the Church

2. The **political kingdom** of the world, governed by the state

We should ask if obeying the state is the will of God. This will only be clear in the **INSTANT OF ACTION** and as an act of faith.

"You can only know what obedience is by obeying. It is no use asking questions; for it is only through obedience that you come to learn the truth" (Dietrich Bonhoeffer, The Cost of discipleship, 1959, p. 68)

"There is no road to faith or discipleship, no other road – only obedience to the call of Jesus" (Dietrich Bonhoeffer, The Cost of discipleship, 1959, p. 49)

Justification for Civil Disobedience

• It is impossible to know whether our actions are truly good or not.

- No amount of human reason can morally justify killing.

- **BONHOEFFER** argues to kill Hitler and disobey the state is only justified by '**bold action as the free response to faith**'. It cannot be justified in ordinary **ETHICAL TERMS**.

- Love is not the only **MORAL PRINCIPLE** by which we can live the moral life. Human ideas **ENSLAVE** humans. Humans are only freed by responding to **GOD'S WILL**.

- Consolation for civil disobedience, such as the assassination attempt on Hitler is possible only through God's promises to forgive the '**man who becomes a sinner in the process**' (Letters and Papers from Prison, p. 138).

- **Duty to God outweighs duty to the State**. Need to break away from Luther's idea of advocating of obedience to civil authority.

- You would be just as guilty for the destruction of a town if you did nothing, as you would be if you were among those who helped to burn it down.

- If you are acting out of love, as Christian ethics demands, you need to **actively challenge injustice and resist it.**

Civil Disobedience - EXAMPLES

- Spoke against Nazi ideas in his **UNIVERSITY** position.

- Spoke against Nazism at **PUBLIC LECTURES**. Banned.

- Criticised **CONFESSING CHURCH** when it wavered under pressure from Hitler to conform.

- Participated in **ILLEGAL SEMINARY** for training pastors.

- Openly spoke about his **PRAYERS** for the defeat of his own country.

- Proclaimed Hitler as the **ANTI-CHRIST** – "therefore we must go on with our work and eliminate him whether he is successful or not" (Kenny et al., Dietrich Bonhoeffer: The Life of a Modern Martyr [Christianity Today Essentials], 2012).

- It is thought he joined the **STAUFFENBERG** plot to **assassinate** Hitler in 1944 (see the film **VALKYRIE)**.

- As a member of the German military intelligence, Bonhoeffer acted as a **DOUBLE AGENT** working with Resistance and Allies.

- Smuggled **JEWS** into Switzerland, posing as agents of military intelligence.

MNEMONIC: Uptown Lads Show Amazing Acrobatics During Summer

Church - Community & Discipline

Like **KANT**, Bonhoeffer believed that a Christian can recognise that they act out of **DUTY** when they act along with the rest of humankind.

- The **MORAL AND SPIRITUAL COMMUNITY** of the Church provide the tools needed to live morally in this world. To do this, the Church needs to become **RELIGIONLESS**.

- The **WORLD COME OF AGE** was costly. In discarding Christian values as 'irrational', **LIBERALISM** brought about the **WESTERN VOID** - a

SPIRITUAL VACUUM that Christianity used to occupy.

- The **NATIONAL SOCIALISM** of the Nazis partly filled this void. Bonhoeffer called for a paradoxical **RELIGIONLESS CHRISTIANITY**.

- The ethical attitudes used by the Church before have no use today and are 'outworn'- represented by Bonhoeffer's metaphor of **RUSTY SWORDS**.

Metaphor of salt and light – visible in the **SERMON ON THE MOUNT**. As salt adds flavour to food, Christians must be present among other people and must act as 'light' for the room in their acting morally.

The Confessing Church

When Christianity and National Socialism were blended, forming the **German Christian movement**, it triggered the founding of the **CONFESSING CHURCH.**

- **1934** – Hitler amended the articles of the **German Evangelical Church** issuing the **ARYAN PARAGRAPH** making it necessary for all clergy to be of Aryan descent.

- **BONHOEFFER** and Martin **NIEMOLLER** disagreed with this change and brought together others who also disagreed. This group formed the early **CONFESSING CHURCH**.

- **1934** – Confessing Church met in **BARMEN** and the foundations of **BARTH'S 'Barmen Declaration'** were formed.

- A Christian's primary **DUTY** is to **CHRIST** and should reject any teaching that is not revealed in Jesus Christ.

Clear denial of Nazi **NATIONAL SOCIALISM** but some say its disobedience against the state was limited and it could have done more politically to aid Jews and other minority groups.

Bonhoeffer tried to take it further to be more inclusive and from this, came his **ECUMENICAL THEOLOGY** – a direct disagreement with the German Christian movement.

In line with 'religionless Christianity', the confessing Church was not to become 'national' – there must be no racial, political, or national boundaries in a Christian community, as Jesus taught. Bonhoeffer – "the Church is her true self when she exists for **HUMANITY**".

Finkenwalde

Following his return from the USA in **1935**, Bonhoeffer was responsible for constructing a community at **FINKENWALDE** for training clergy for the Confessing Church.

Nazi control of the German Church and the appointment of a **REICH BISHOP** led to a decline in suitable clergy. The **HIMMLER DECREE** of **1937** made the training of clergy for the Confessing Church illegal and Finkenwalde was shut down by the **THIRD REICH** in September.

The **VIRTUE OF DISCIPLINE** was thought to be the most practical of the Christian virtues and Finkenwalde was intended as a place to develop this through practical Christian living. Key features are listed below:

- **Discipline** - Life was basic and monastic. Both the body and the mind needed to be disciplined and well exercised. The group frequently went on long bike rides together.

- **Meditation** - Foundation of prayer, develops discipline.

- **Community for others -** No one is perfect and so the Church is not one for the righteous but one for the forgiven. Needs to be 'outward looking' – Christ dies for all, not just for Christians.

- **Bible** - Heart of daily life for a Christian. An intelligent understanding of the development of Christian teaching was encouraged by debate and discussion.

- **Brotherhood** - Love of and for Christ binds together the community, sustained by the Holy Spirit. Former students to be kept informed of developments and director should change often so that the group does not become 'stuck in its ways'.

MNEMONIC: Dancing Makes Cate's Brothers Bop

The Cost Of Discipleship

Bonhoeffer's teaching on Ethics as action

Christianity is grounded in the **EVERYDAY WORLD** – it is not an 'otherworldly institution'. This is affirmed in God's **INCARNATION** – where he took on human flesh, became man and lived among humankind.

Rather than investigating God's nature as human/ Divine, we should be asking **'who is Christ for us today?'**

Bonhoeffer was influenced by Karl Barth, a Swiss **CALVINIST** theologian. The meaning of Christianity is in action.

BARTH - we do not know God – it is God who chooses to reveal Himself to humans – always a special and never a general act. **BONHOEFFER**

agrees but says we should be careful not to accept the limited role of 'passively receiving' revelation – **we must 'do' as well as 'hear' the law** - E.g. Pharisees listened to commands but did not act on God's behalf; and in Luke, Martha acts but fails to listen to Jesus' teaching.

CONSCIENCE is the experience of disunity in the self – it prompts action. Ethics is action. Action is liberating.

Costly Grace

"When Christ calls a man, he bids him come and die...Suffering then, is the badge of true discipleship" (Bonhoeffer, The Cost of Discipleship, 1959, p. 79, p., 80)

Authentic Christianity must be based on:

• **CHRIST**

• **SCRIPTURE**

• **FAITH**

These are the three fundamentals. If we stray from these, then we only have human intervention and nothing else. Religion as an institution is a human invention - like politics.

Church must be **SEPARATE** from State if it is to avoid being politically manipulated.

In taking on the world, the Christian disciple endangers himself.

CHEAP GRACE e.g. rituals, cannot win God's grace. Rather, grace is 'costly'.

"Costly because it costs man his life, and it is grace because it gives man the only true life ... Above all, it is costly because it cost God the life of his Son" (The Cost of Discipleship, p. 5).

Grace is 'freely given' by God, not earned. However, it should not be 'cheap' and taken for granted, under the cheap umbrella that Jesus died and saved us from our sins - so we take the grace but avoid the cost. Churches are in danger of offering grace without the discipleship.

"Cheap grace is effectively a lie, it is not the grace of God but a self-congratulating grace we give ourselves" (Ahluwalia & Bowie, 2016, p. 421)

COSTLY GRACE for Bonhoeffer involved a realisation he might have to die, though he did not seek to suffer and never saw himself as a martyr.

Letters from Prison – affirmed the Christian life, standing against all things evil. He did not dwell on suffering.

Against injustice - Jesus was '**the man for others**' and so the Church as Christ's body must also be a Church for others. It was failing.

Sacrifice & Suffering

The Cross embodies the suffering of Christ and in human suffering, Christianity engages with the world reflected in this Cross of suffering.

God, too, suffers in Jesus, acting in solidarity with humankind.

• **KRISIS** (Barth's use of NT Greek) – judgement, decision, verdict.

• **PARADOX** – God reveals His 'crisis' (judgement, redemption) in response to 'crisis' of the world (sinfulness etc.)

THEOLOGY OF CRISIS - Crisis of human sinfulness can only be triumphed by God's judgement and faith in His redemption through Jesus Christ.

The **Passion of Jesus Christ** – his sufferings leading up to and including his death are linked to the call to **DISCIPLESHIP**. 'Those who would come after me must leave self behind, take up their **CROSS** and follow me!" (Mark 8:34) Jesus died without admiration or honour, 'a man of **SORROWS** and acquainted with grief' (Isaiah 53).

Being a disciple means 'picking up the cross' and so suffering and sacrifice are an inherent aspect of the nature of discipleship.

Solidarity

Solidarity with the Jews - Bonhoeffer wrote his essay '**The Church and the Jewish Question'** in response to the boycott of Jewish business in April **1933**. Called for solidarity of those afflicted by Nazism.

Publicly rejected the claim that punishment of the Jews was God's work for their rejection of Christ. Called it **GODLESS VIOLENCE**– in response to **NIGHT OF BROKEN GLASS (KRISTELNACHT) 1938.**

Living the '**Christian life**' is not to 'become religious' but to be there for other people, sharing in their experiences in a form of **TRANSCENDENCE**.

Q. DOES BONHOEFFER PLACE TOO MUCH EMPHASIS ON SUFFERING?

YES	NO
Bonhoeffer's own experience of suffering is not representative of all Christian experience.	Bonhoeffer's teaching on suffering and discipleship is dependent on **INJUSTICE** and suffering existing - which it does still today.
It seems **IMPOSSIBLE** to live a Christian life of discipleship involving suffering and sacrifice if you live in a place of peace and justice	Everyone experiences suffering in some form at some point in their lives.
Bonhoeffer seems to downplay the **JOY** and **HOPE** offered by the Resurrection. Jesus' Passion reaches beyond his suffering – the Resurrection represents a triumph over death and sin.	Bonhoeffer focuses on solidarity as well as suffering – people might feel **CONSOLATION** as a result of this.
	Passing through the cross rather than trying to avoid the suffering, is a necessary part of following the call of Jesus. Christians should be more **ENGAGED** - as Jesus was.

Q. DOES BONHOEFFER HAVE RELEVANCE TODAY?

YES	NO
Could lead people to a more meaningful life in today's materialistic world if people do abandon self-interest, and 'take up their **CROSS**'.	Pressures on Church to **MODERNISE** seems to conflict with Bonhoeffer's focus on following God's commands alone.
SOLIDARITY with the poor will always be a relevant message.	Obedience to God's and not state law could cause further **CONFLICT** today in light of religious conflict.
Gives a place to Christianity as a spiritual **CONSCIENCE** in state's involvement with politics of the world.	Decision to support assassination goes against Martin Luther King's **PASSIVE RESISTANCE** which is a more powerful way.

Q. CAN BONHOEFFER'S ETHICS ADDRESS GLOBAL POLITICS?

YES	NO
STANLEY HAUERWAS – Bonhoeffer's care for truth in politics is a much-needed challenge to pragmatism of democracy in the West.	Only works in similar circumstance to Nazism within which Bonhoeffer was operating - extremes of **GENOCIDE**.
Christian Church has a special role to play – tolerance should not replace **ENGAGEMENT WITH TRUTH** as this leads to indifference and cynicism and as Bonhoeffer said, a 'void' that can be filled with all sorts of tyranny.	He only compromised Christian pacifism because of the extreme circumstance.
Ethics targeted at a singular threat – Nazism. Today, there is more threat - **ISIS.**	Theology is not best placed to handle **COMPLEX ISSUES** in liberal democratic societies.

Q. ARE BONHOEFFER'S ETHICS COMPATIBLE WITH PLURAL MORAL SOCIETIES?

YES	NO
Joseph Fletcher interpreted Bonhoeffer as tolerant of other people's **RELATIVISTIC** morals only so far as they do not pose harm to others.	Bonhoeffer's ethics remind moral pluralism that trying to be non-judgemental of various moral viewpoints loses sight of what it means to be a **JUST** community.
Judging killing of an innocent as right or wrong is relative to the principle of Christian **LOVE**.	Fletcher is misguided in his interpretation of Bonhoeffer – Bonhoeffer was **NOT** a moral relativist.
Telling the truth is also relative. According to Fletcher, Bonhoeffer "is as **RADICAL** a version of the situational method as any Christian relativist could call for" (**Situation Ethics**).	Christian ethics formed outside of secular society and **FUNDAMENTALLY OPPOSED** to it. "Render to Caesar the things that are Caesar's" may be Jesus' judgement on Caesar's **IDOLATRY**.
Bonhoeffer appears to make judgements **SITUATIONALLY** and not **UNCONDITIONALLY**. Yet perhaps the Bible does the same eg 'thou shalt not kill' does not include killing in war and self-defence.	Truth is **ABSOLUTE** but through faith and conscience, is applied in each situation. For Bonhoeffer, relativizing moral values undermines truth itself.

Q. ARE BONHOEFFER'S THEOLOGICAL ETHICS COMPATIBLE WITH MULTI-FAITH SOCIETIES?

YES	NO
AFTER TEN YEARS – an essay written to his co-conspirators – recognises that sympathy is not just tolerance but is a real experience of what it is like to belong to an oppressed faith community or part of the dominant group, the source of power.	Despite Bonhoeffer's best efforts to save the oppressed Jews, he still maintained that they should still **CONVERT** to Christianity eventually.
Some might say that Bonhoeffer's **COSTLY GRACE** is better equipped to manage the growing multi-faith dimension of the West, appreciating its sacrifices; a practical approach to questioning power without losing integrity as Christ's witness.	Perhaps this makes his theology incompatible with the **MULTI-FAITH** community of the Western world; despite his emphasis that the state should give equal rights and protection to **ALL** its citizens.

Strengths

1. Bonhoeffer's focus on **SHARED REFLECTION** and reading of Scripture, alongside shared living and community provide a good basis for understanding the Scripture and not just choosing parts of it.

2. A **COMMUNAL** approach could discourage distorted understanding of God's will.

3. Bonhoeffer's account of true Christianity and what was wrong with the German Christians being misled by the Nazi-Controlled German Church would seem **ACCURATE** and attract sympathy today.

4. Calls into question the nature of civic authorities and what they are doing – Bonhoeffer proposed an **ETHIC OF ACTION**.

Weaknesses

1. Interpreting God's will might be **MISTAKEN**.

2. It is not always clear how God will want us to act in any given situation - requires God-like **WISDOM.**

3. If someone has a distorted view of God's will, Bonhoeffer's teaching could be **DANGEROUS** and even support genocide as in the book of **JOSHUA** where entire peoples were wiped out in cities of Jericho and Ai.

4. St Paul's Romans 13:1-2 suggests that **OBEDIENCE** to the state is important as state leaders have been established by God. Bonhoeffer differs from this.

5. Even Jesus did not openly challenge the rule of **PONTIUS PILATE**

and he did not encourage people not to pay their taxes, even though he did challenge religious authorities and social norms. Contrast with the **ZEALOTS** who fostered a disastrous rebellion against Rome in **66AD**.

Possible Exam Questions

1. "Using the will of God as a guide for moral behaviour is impractical, as in most circumstances it is impossible to know what god wants us to do." Discuss.

2. To what extent, if at all, does the theology of Bonhoeffer have relevance for Christians today?

3. "Bonhoeffer's most important teaching is on leadership." Discuss.

4. "Christian ethics means being obedient to god's will." Discuss.

5. To what extent was Bonhoeffer's religious community at Finkenwalde successful?

Key Quotes

1. "Whoever wishes to take up the problem of a Christian ethic must ... ask 'what is the will of God?'" Dietrich Bonhoeffer, Ethics, p. 161.

2. "The nature of this will of God can only be clear in the moment of action"." Dietrich Bonhoeffer, No Rusty Swords, p. 43.

3. "For the sake of Christ, the worldly order is subject to the commandment of God...There exists, therefore, a Christian responsibility for secular institutions,". Dietrich Bonhoeffer: Ethics (1955/2005), p. 289

4. "We make again and again the surprising and terrifying discovery that the will of God does not reveal itself before our eyes as clearly as we had hoped." Dietrich Bonhoeffer: No Rusty Swords (1965), p. 46

5. "And Jesus answering said unto them, Render to Caesar the things that are Caesar's, and to God the things that are God's. And they marvelled at him." Mark 12:17

6. "Let everyone be subject to the governing authorities, for there is no authority except that which God has established. The authorities that exist have been established by God." Romans 13:1

7. "Costly because it costs man his life, and it is grace because it gives man the only true life ... Above all, it is costly because it cost God the life of his Son' (The Cost of Discipleship, p. 5).

8. "There is no road to faith or discipleship, no other road – only obedience to the call of Jesus" (Dietrich Bonhoeffer, The Cost of discipleship, 1959, p. 49)

9. "The followers are a visible community; their discipleship visible in action which lifts them out of the world" Dietrich Bonhoeffer, The Cost of Discipleship, 1959, p. 106

10. "Who will speak up for those who are voiceless?" Psalm 31:8

11. "When Christ calls a man, he bids him come and die...Suffering then, is the badge of true discipleship" (Bonhoeffer, The Cost of Discipleship, 1959, p. 79, p., 80)

Book 3
Ethics Year 1

OCR Revision Guide (New Spec)

Completely Revised

Peter Baron

The Examination

The OCR Year 1 Ethics Course narrows the applied topics down to two - euthanasia and business ethics, whilst retaining emphasis on the key moral theories of Utilitarianism, Situation Ethics, Kantian ethics and Natural Law. We are required to apply Natural Law and Situation Ethics to issues surrounding euthanasia, and Kant and Utilitarianism to business ethics.

- **CASE STUDIES** are an excellent way of thinking through issues surrounding applied ethics - such as Diane Pretty in 2002 (euthanasia) or Enron in 2003 (business ethics). You will find these on the website www.peped.org

- **MAPPING THE THEORIES** gives a sequence of thought which goes from a starting point (such as **SYNDERESIS** for Natural Law) to a finishing point (**EUDAIMONIA** for Natural Law) and then links the concepts together to form an analysis.

- **TEXTBOOKS** may have their place, but you are examined on the syllabus alone, so study it carefully. There are many ways of doing and thinking about ethics. Wilcockson and Wilkinson (2016) frequently take a Roman Catholic perspective (eg quotes from encyclicals and the Catholic Catechism). But you could just as well quote from the Church of England, the United Reformed Church or the Baptist or Orthodox churches to gain a Christian perspective. Or line up a humanist or atheist perspective against it. Textbooks also include extra material which is not strictly necessary to be an A grade candidate.

Introduction to Ethics

Key Terms

- **NORMATIVE ETHICS** - how norms (values of good and bad) are derived and then applied to the real world.

- **META-ETHICS** - the meaning and function of ethical language.

- **OBJECTIVE TRUTH -** the view that truth is testable by observation and experience.

- **RELATIVISM** - the view that all values (norms) are simply expressions of culture and there are no universal, unchanging values of 'good'.

- **SUBJECTIVE TRUTH** - the view that truth is something that depends on an individual perception or belief system and cannot be shared objectively.

- **SITUATION ETHICS** - a theory of ethics that holds that what is good or bad needs to be assessed according to what maximises love in any situation.

- **TELEOLOGICAL ETHICS** - ethics that focuses on the end or telos of an action, for example, Situation Ethics focuses on love as the highest end or purpose.

- **DEONTOLOGICAL** - ethics that focuses on the duty (deon) or rule.

Normative Ethics

Asks the question "how should I act, morally speaking?" or "what ought I to do?"

A norm is a "value" i.e. something I think of as good. The normative theories we study at AS or Year 1 (OCR) are: Natural Law, Kantian ethics, Utilitarianism and Situation Ethics. Each theory derives the idea of goodness a different way: Natural Law with reference to the true rational purpose of human beings; Utilitarianism, with reference to the one assumed norm of happiness and its maximisation; Kantian ethics, by an a priori method of taking an imaginative step backwards and universalising our action; and Situation Ethics by maximising the one norm of love in a given situation.

Meta-Ethics

Meta-ethics studies the foundations of ethics and meaning of ethical terms (what does it mean to say something is good?). It particularly focuses on ethical language. Meta-ethics is studied at **A2** level. Key meta-ethical questions include:

- "Is morality absolute – applying everywhere and for all time, or is it relative, specific to a time and place – a culture, situation or viewpoint?"

- "Is there such a thing as a moral fact?"

- "What do different ethical theorists mean by 'good'?"

- "Is goodness a natural feature of the world to be accessed and measured (a bit like science)?"

Applied Ethics

Applies ethical theories to real world situations. The applied issues at AS or Year 1 (OCR) are:

- **Euthanasia applied to Natural Law and Situation Ethics**

- **Business Ethics applied to Utilitarianism and Kantian ethics.**

A key question in applied ethics is: how do I apply the norm derived by any one ethical theory to the issues surrounding euthanasia and business ethics? The syllabus helps us identify these issues: sanctity of human life, quality of life and autonomy for euthanasia, and globalisation, whistle-blowing, and the interests of stakeholders for business ethics. We could also add our own, such as slippery slope arguments in euthanasia and environmental responsibility for business.

Moreover, we can ask the question generally: is there any difference between an **ACT** (doing something deliberately) and an **OMISSION** (failing to do something)? For example, in cases of euthanasia is failing to offer life support the same ethically as deliberately administering a drug that will kill?

Deontological

Acts are right or wrong in themselves (intrinsically) – it is not about consequences. Often stresses the rules or duty (Kantian ethics is pure deontology and Natural Law has both teleological and deontological aspects). **DEON** is Greek for duty.

Teleological

Teleological theories (**TELOS** = end in Greek) focuses on the purpose and consequences of actions. An action is good only if it brings about beneficial consequences and so fulfils the good purpose (it is instrumentally good, not intrinsically because actions are means to some other end like happiness or pleasure), for example, Utilitarianism (good purpose is maximising happiness) and Situation Ethics (good purpose is maximising agape love). Joseph Fletcher declares: "the end justifies the means, nothing else".

Four Questions To Ask Of Ethical Theories

- **Derivation**: How does the moral theory derive (produce) the idea of goodness?

- **Application**: How can we apply the "good" to choices we make, such as Natural Law to euthanasia or Kantian ethics to business?

- **Realism**: How realistic is the theory with reference to human psychology and our own experience?

- **Motivation**: Why should I be moral? How does this ethical theory suggest I should be motivated to save a stranger in need? What stops me living my life as an ethical egoist, just putting my self-interest first?

These questions will be answered for all moral theories in the final chapter.

Key Quotes - Norms

1. "There are no absolute universal moral standards binding on all men at all times". John Ladd

2. "All men are created equal..they are endowed with certain unalienable rights". US Declaration of Independence

3. "Values are merely culturally approved habits". Ruth Benedict

4. "In its nature, the moral judgement is wholly independent of religion". William Temple

5. "The end justifies the means, nothing else". Joseph Fletcher

6. "There is no objective truth". J.L.Mackie

7. "We are in danger of falling into a tyranny of relativism". Pope Benedict

8. "The only good thing is the good will". Immanuel Kant

9. "There could still be a set of general moral norms applicable to all cultures and even recognised in most, which a culture could disregard at its own expense". Louis Pojman

10. "The Gentiles have the law written on their hearts, to which their conscience bears witness". Romans 2:14

Natural Law

A normative **DEONTOLOGICAL** theory coming from a **TELEOLOGICAL** worldview, as Aristotle argues that the good is defined by the **RATIONAL ENDS** or **FINAL CAUSES** which people by nature pursue.

"Natural Law is the sharing in the eternal law by intelligent creatures" argues **AQUINAS** and calls these rational ends **OBJECTS OF THE WILL**. Key assumptions are that we have a fixed human nature, there is an eternal law in God himself, and the **SYNDERESIS** principle – that all human beings naturally share a conscience that guides us to "do good and avoid evil". Aquinas calls synderesis "the first principle of the natural law" and it is one of two words he uses for conscience.

Key Terms

- **NATURAL LAW** - "right reason in agreement with nature", (Cicero). "The sharing in the eternal law by rational creatures', (Aquinas).

- **SYNDERESIS** - the first principle that we by nature seek to do good and avoid evil – or have an innate knowledge of first principles (the primary precepts). This makes the theory universal in application (it applies to a Christian believer and a non-believer or believer of another religion).

- **PRIMARY PRECEPTS** - principles known innately which define the rational ends or goods of human existence and define the good goals we pursue - these are general and do not change.

- **SECONDARY PRECEPTS** - applications of the primary precepts using human reason, which are not absolute and so may change. For example, Pope Francis has given hints that the Catholic church may revise its absolute ban on contraception as a violation of the primary precept of reproduction.

- **APPARENT GOODS** - acts done from reason which do not correspond to the natural law.

- **REAL GOODS** - acts done from human reason which correspond to the natural law.

- **NATURAL RIGHTS** - rights given to human beings because of their very nature as human. These are enshrined in the US Declaration of Independence which starts: 'we hold these rights to be inalienable'.

- **ETERNAL LAW** - the law as conceived by God and existing as an ideal of all law and projected in the design of the Universe.

- **DIVINE LAW** - the law revealed to humankind in the Bible, such as the ten commandments in the book of Exodus or the beatitudes in Matthew.

- **HUMAN LAW** - the laws we establish by human reason as our social laws.

Synderesis: 'each precious child, born with the desire to do good, and avoid evil'

Aquinas' Argument

AQUINAS sought to reconcile Christian thought with Greek thinking (**ARISTOTLE**'s works) discovered in Islamic libraries at the **FALL OF TOLEDO** (1085), when Christian armies reconquered Spain.

He sees goodness in the **DIVINE ESSENCE** (nature of God) which has a purpose – the **ETERNAL LAW** – reflected in our **HUMAN NATURE** and the ends we rationally pursue. A key assumption Aquinas makes is called the **SYNDERESIS** principle that we naturally "do good and avoid evil" – which is the opposite of the **REFORMATION** assumption that "all have sinned and fall short of God's glory" (Romans 3:23).

We are born with good natures, able to reason and so pursue good ends or objects of the will. The **DIVINE LAW** reflects God's eternal law and is revealed in holy Scripture (eg Ten Commandments of Exodus 20). From

207

these observable God-designed rational ends (goals) we get the **PRIMARY PRECEPTS**.

Primary Precepts

There are five observable "goods" or rational ends we pursue. (Acronym **POWER**).

- **P**reservation of life

- **O**rdered society

- **W**orship of God

- **E**ducation and

- **R**eproduction

These reflect the **DIVINE WILL** because God designed us with a rational nature in His image. Notice that **VERITATIS SPLENDOR** (1995 Papal document) has subtly changed these – Worship of God becomes **APPRECIATION OF BEAUTY** (to fit with our agnostic age), and it adds concern for the environment to reflect the new emphasis on stewardship rather than **DOMINION** (Genesis 1:24 "and let man have dominion over the earth"). Note that the commitment to environmental value is weak in Veritatis Splendor: "to preserve and cultivate the riches of the natural world'. These subtle changes may indicate that Natural Law is not as **ABSOLUTE** as we sometimes think. The fourth type of law is **HUMAN LAW**.

For society to flourish (Greek telos (purpose) of **EUDAIMONIA** sees happiness as personal and social flourishing) we need to bring our human law in line with the **ETERNAL LAW** of God, or put another way, make it appropriate for rational human beings to fulfil their Godly destiny – being with God forever, and being Christlike.

The Four Laws

Natural Law can be mapped in two ways. The first way is **TELEOLOGICAL**   because it focuses on the end or telos of human behaviour - to achieve a flourishing or fulfilled life, **EUDAIMONIA** (see mindmap). Aristotle begins Nichomachean Ethcis by arguing 'the intrinsic good is that at which all things aim' - a broad and general goal.

The second way is by focusing on duties created by the four laws.

- **ETERNAL LAW** - a blueprint in the mind of God of the principles by which God made and controls the universe, which we discover by observation **A POSTERIORI** - through scientific experiments for example, or **A PRIORI** by pure reason as in Mathematics.

- **NATURAL LAW** - the moral law inherent in human beings, discoverable by reason, and expressed in the rational goals which humans by nature pursue.

- **DIVINE LAW** - expressed in the Bible (eg the Ten Commandments or Sermon on the Mount) and then interpreted and applied by human reason.

- **HUMAN LAW** - formulated as codes that create the common good and the precept of an ordered society, and should reflect the eternal law in order to be seen to be good and just. If a ruler ordered that we kill all female babies this would be bad for human flourishing and contrary to the **PRMARY PRECEPT** of preservation of life. and so an unjust and 'bad' law.

These can be represented as a diamond with eternal law at the top. Note that we 'are only required to obey secular rulers to the extent that justice requires' (Aquinas). Evil laws should be resisted and disobeyed.

Secondary Precepts

These are **APPLICATIONS** of the **PRIMARY PRECEPTS** and may change eg as our society changes, science advances our understanding of the Divine Mind, or a situation demands it (eg Thou shalt not kill gets suspended in times of war).

Aquinas suggests **POLYGAMY** (many wives) may sometimes be justified. We don't necessarily have to accept Roman Catholic applications eg Abortion is tantamount to murder, Euthanasia breaks the **SANCTITY OF LIFE**, contraception goes against the primary natural purpose of sex, which is **REPRODUCTION**, and homosexual behaviour is described as **INTRINSICALLY DISORDERED** (the phrase used in **HUMANAE VITAE**, 1968).

There is another assumption here, that there is one human nature – heterosexual- and so there can't be a gay nature. Modern Psychology (eg Carl **JUNG**) suggests we have male and female aspects to our natures and Chinese philosophy has always talked in terms of **YING** and **YANG** – the two aspects of our nature.

Phronesis

Practical wisdom (phronesis in Greek) is important because we need to cultivate right judgment to identify the non-absolute **SECONDARY PRECEPTS**. "Practical wisdom requires the application to action, which is the goal of practical reason" (Aquinas). So Natural Law has a situational aspect - we need to assess and 'the more specific the conditions are, the greater the probability of an exception arising', argues Aquinas (ST I -II q.94 a.4c). **SYNDERESIS** gives us a general orientation towards the good but **PHRONESIS** fills in the details of how to apply any primary precept.

Apparent Goods

We cannot consciously sin because our nature is such that we believe we are "doing good and avoiding evil" – the **SYNDERESIS** principle – even when practising genocide. However, though we rationalise it, this clearly breaks the **ETERNAL LAW** reflected in the **NATURAL LAW** that most rational humans want to **PRESERVE LIFE** (primary precept **P** of **POWER** acronym above). We cannot flourish if we break the Natural Law – in this sense we are being sub-human and irrational (even though we believe otherwise). **AQUINAS** calls these **APPARENT GOODS** – which we mistakenly believe (eg Hitler's genocide) are **REAL GOODS**. We can sin, but not consciously, which is why Evangelical Christians dislike Natural Law theory – arguing it is unrealistic (our very reason is distorted by sin) and unbiblical (it seems to deny Paul's teaching on **ORIGINAL SIN**, inherited from Adam after the **FALL** in Genesis 3).

Two Goods In Conflict

In business ethics the principles of truthfulness and loyalty to the company come into conflict when a whistleblower discovers evidence of wrongdoing, or with euthanasia, when doctors increase the morphine dose to alleviate pain in the knowledge that they will kill the patient. **DOUBLE EFFECT** argues that if the primary effect results from a good intention (alleviate suffering) then the secondary effect isn't evil (causing a death). Notice you can only make the judgement by considering **CONSEQUENCES** and the end of patient welfare. Aquinas argues: "moral actions take their character from what is intended" and so if I act in self defence and unintentionally kill someone I am not doing wrong as long as the action is **PROPORTIONATE.**

Strengths

AUTONOMOUS AND RATIONAL: Natural law is an autonomous, rational theory and it is wrong to say that you have to believe in God to make sense of it. Aquinas speaks of "the pattern of life lived according to reason". You could be a Darwinian atheist and believe in natural law derived by empirical observation, with the primary precept of survival (Aquinas' preservation of life). Richard **DAWKINS** (The Selfish Gene) goes so far as to argue for a natural genetic tendency to be altruistic: a lust to be nice. "The theory of Natural Law suggests..morality is **AUTONOMOUS**. It has its own questions, its own methods of answering them, and its own standards of truth, and religious considerations are not the point". Rachels (2006:56)

AN EXALTED VIEW OF HUMAN BEINGS: We use reason to work out how to live. So we are not slaves to our passions or our genes. Natural

Law has a purpose: a flourishing society and a person fulfilled and happy - **EUDAIMONIA**. It is not ultimately about restricting us by rules, but setting us free to fulfil our proper purpose or **TELOS**, inherent in our design: to rationally assent to personal growth. If we can agree on our purpose we can agree on what morality is for. Moreover, we don't have to accept the fact/value division inherent in Moore or Ayer's philosophy. "The natural world is not to be regarded merely as a realm of facts, devoid of value or purpose. Instead, the world is conceived to be a **RATIONAL ORDER** with value and purpose built into its very nature". Rachels (2006: 50)

FLEXIBLE: Natural Law is not inflexible. The primary precepts may be general and unchanging, but as Aquinas argued, **SECONDARY PRECEPTS** can change depending on circumstances, culture and worldview. Aquinas calls them 'proximate conclusions of reason'. The Doctrine of **DOUBLE EFFECT** is also a way to escape the moral dilemmas which exist when two rules conflict, (See Louis Pojman 2006: 47-51) – so not as **ABSOLUTE** as textbooks suggest.

Weaknesses

A FIXED HUMAN NATURE: Aquinas believes in one fixed, shared human nature with certain natural properties eg heterosexual. But evidence suggests there are gay genes and so there is no one natural human nature, but many. This is actually a form of the **NATURALISTIC FALLACY**, the movement from an "is" to an "ought". "It may be that sex does produce babies, but it does not follow that sex ought or ought not to be engaged in only for that purpose. Facts are one thing, values are another". Rachels (2006:52)

AN OPTIMISTIC VIEW: Aquinas believes that we **INNATELY** (we are born with) have a "tendency to do good and avoid evil", **SYNDERESIS**. This is in contrast with Augustine who believes that, due to the Fall, we are born into sin, the sin of Adam, or perhaps the view of psychologists like Freud, that natural selfishness becomes moralised by upbringing and socialisation.

IMMORAL OUTCOMES: Natural Law has been interpreted to ban contraception, because this interferes with the natural primary precept of reproduction. But a. it's not clear that sex is exclusively for reproduction, in fact, the function of bonding may be primary and b. the consequence of this policy in Africa has had evil effects of the spread of **AIDS** and the birth of **AIDS** infected children who often become orphans living on the streets.

Possible Exam Questions

1. "Natural Law does not present a helpful method for making moral decisions". Discuss

2. "Moral decisions should be based on duty, not purpose". Assess with reference to the theory of Natural Law.

3. "Human beings are born with the tendency to pursue morally good ends". Evaluate in the light of teleological aspects of Natural Law.

4. "Explain and justify the doctrine of double effect with reference to an ethical dilemma of your choice concerning euthanasia".

Key Quotes - Natural Law

1. "The natural law is the sharing in the eternal law by intelligent creatures". Thomas Aquinas

2. "For Aquinas, the basis of the moral life is prudence, right practical reason in the pursuit of charity". Herbert McCabe

3. "The order of the precepts of the natural law is the order of our natural inclinations". Thomas Aquinas

4. "Our ultimate end is unrelated good, namely God, who alone can fill our will to the brim because of infinite goodness". Thomas Aquinas

5. "The natural law is unchangeable in its first principles, but in its secondary principles it may be changed through some special causes hindering the following of the primary precepts". Thomas Aquinas

6. "The natural law involves universality as it is inscribed in the rational nature of a person. It makes itself felt in every person endowed with reason". Veritatis Splendor (1995)

7. "Every marital act must of necessity retain its intrinsic relationship to the procreation of human life". Humanae Vitae (1968)

8. "The theory of Natural law suggests morality is autonomous. It has its own questions, its own methods of answering them and its own standards of truth. Religious considerations are not the point". James Rachels

9. "The world is conceived as a rational order with value and purpose built into its very nature". James Rachels

10. "Nature inclines to that which is necessary for the perfection of community". Thomas Aquinas

Confusions - Natural Law

1. "Natural" means "as we see in the natural world". This isn't true because many things we see in the natural world we would argue are immoral (eg killing the weak which animals do all the time). "Natural" means something closer to "**APPROPRIATE** for our rational human nature", for example, we may naturally feel lust but it is irrational and wrong to seek to indulge this lust with a complete stranger.

2. "Natural law is dogmatic and inflexible". This is a wrong reading of Aquinas who himself argues that the **SECONDARY PRECEPTS** are liable to change with circumstances and our developed understanding. It is quite possible to be a Natural Law theorist and argue in favour of contraception on the grounds that it is necessary to save lives and reduce destructive population growth. Roman Catholic interpretations are open to debate.

3. "Natural Law is deontological". This is an overstatement as Natural Law is profoundly teleological in its goal of eudaimonia and follows the Greek teleological wordlview. However, it is still law, and is enshrined in principles and rules and codes of law which should reflect the **ETERNAL LAW** of God. The laws have to be **JUST** and subject to right reason.

4. "Natural Law requires God". Aquinas rejects **DIVINE COMMAND THEORY** (the argument that something is good or bad because God commands it). Natural Law therefore does not require God but is knowable by reason alone and observable in nature. Christian Natural Law theory argues that the divine blueprint for the Universe is reflected in its design and discoverable by scientific research, as well as reflection on the proper rational purposes of human beings.

Kantian Ethics

Key Terms

- **AUTONOMY** freedom to reason about the moral law

- **CATEGORICAL** unconditional, absolute, with no 'ifs"

- **HYPOTHETICAL** conditional, relative to circumstances, with 'ifs'

- **SUMMUM BONUM** the greatest good, combining virtue and happiness

- **DUTY** the sole moral motive of pursuing a line of action because it is right, whether or not we feel like it

Deontological

A **NORMATIVE** theory (tells you what is right and wrong/what you ought to do), that is **DEONTOLOGICAL** (acts are intrinsically right and wrong in themselves, stressing rules and duties), **ABSOLUTIST** (applies universally in all times, places, situations) and is **A PRIORI** (derived from reason alone, not experience).

Autonomy

The key Kantian assumption is that we are **AUTONOMOUS** moral agents (self-ruled) which have free choice and free reason, rather than **HETERONOMOUS** meaning "ruled by others", where the others could be God, your peer group, or the Church. Kant adopted the **ENLIGHTENMENT** slogan "dare to reason" and was awakened out of his slumbers by reading Jean-Jacques **ROUSSEAU**'s theory of the social contract.

Good Will

Kant argues that the only thing that is morally good without exception is the **GOOD WILL**. A person of good will is someone motivated by **DUTY** alone. They are not motivated by self-interest, happiness or a feeling of sympathy. The good will is an **INTRINSIC** good (it is good in itself and not as a means to something else) and it doesn't matter if it doesn't bring about good consequences. Even if the good will achieved nothing good – even if it were combined with all manner of other evils – "it would shine forth like a jewel, having full value in itself". He contrasts this with other qualities (such as courage) which **CAN** be good but might also be bad depending on the situation (eg a courageous suicide bomber) which are **EXTRINSIC** goods as they depend on the circumstances.

Duty

Kant argues that we must follow our duty. It is not about what we want to do (our **INCLINATIONS**) or what will lead to the best consequences: only the action which springs from duty is a moral action. Doing your duty (eg helping a beggar) may be pleasurable, but this cannot be the reason why you did your duty (the **MOTIVE**). For it to be moral you have to act because it is your duty, and **FOR NO OTHER REASON**.

Categorical Imperative (C.I.)

How do you know what your duty is? Kant argues that this comes from the **CATEGORICAL IMPERATIVE**. It is categorical because it applies to us universally – simply because we have rational wills. By contrast a **HYPOTHETICAL IMPERATIVE** takes the form "If you want X, then you must do Y" (eg if you want to lose weight, then you must stop eating so much). The difference is the categorical imperative applies to us unconditionally, without any reference to a goal we might have (it is simply the form "You must do Y").

C.I. 1 THE FORMULA OF LAW

"So act that the maxim of your action may be willed as a universal law for all humanity". For any action to be moral, you must be able to **CONSISTENTLY UNIVERSALISE** it. For example, if you decide not to keep a promise, then you must be able to consistently imagine a world where **EVERYONE** doesn't keep their promises – something Kant thought was impossible (because then no-one would believe a promise and so promise-keeping would vanish). He calls this a **CONTRADICTION IN NATURE** because the very nature of the thing – promising – is destroyed and so the action becomes self-contradictory.

C.I. 2 FORMULA OF ENDS

"Never treat people simply as a means to an end but always also as an end in themselves". People are **RATIONAL** and **AUTONOMOUS** (self-legislators) and so are worthy of respect. We cannot ONLY use them as a means for getting something else, but always as rational beings with dignity. We universalise our common humanity – which means we treat others as equals, with rights.

Kant imagines a community of purely rational agents, each of whom is a **LEGISLATOR** (someone who decides laws) and a **SUBJECT** (someone who has to follow those laws) in what he calls a **KINGDOM OF ENDS**. We can only act on moral laws that would be accepted by this fully rational community – we belong to a moral parliament where we are free participators in the law-making process. This introduces an important **SOCIAL** aspect to Kantian ethics. "Kantian ethics is the ethics of democracy". James Rachels

Summum Bonum

The **SUMMUM BONUM** or "supreme good" is **VIRTUE** (a person of 'good will' who follows their duty by applying the Categorical Imperative) combined with **HAPPINESS**. We should not act in order to get happiness (because moral action should only involve doing our duty for duty's sake), but the ideal is that we should be happy to the degree that we **DESERVE** to be happy. This is obviously not something that can be found in this life – we see bad people living happy lives and good people living unhappy lives – therefore the Summum Bonum must be able to be achieved in the **AFTERLIFE**.

Three Postulates

Kant argued there are three necessary postulates (or propositions) for morality:

1. **FREEDOM** (we must be free to make moral decisions)

2. **IMMORTALITY** (there must be an afterlife in order to achieve the summum bonum).

3. **GOD** (necessary to guarantee the moral law and to judge fairly and reward or punish).

Strengths Of Kant

It's **REASONABLE** – pretty much what most people consider morality to be about (ie universalising your behaviour). The various formulations of the Categorical Imperative take the **DIGNITY** and **EQUALITY** of human beings very seriously. The innocent are protected by the universal equality given to all human beings.

Weaknesses

It is **INFLEXIBLE** as absolutes have to be applied in all situations irrespective of what we consider to be the wisest choice. Kant also seems to make a clear distinction between our **EMOTIONS** and the ethical choice done from duty alone - but is it really morally doubtful if I act out of emotion like compassion and not just from **DUTY** alone? Also, what happens when two duties **CONFLICT** (eg I need to lie to a crazy knifeman who is enquiring if my friend is in the house - Kant's own example where he insists we tell the truth whatever happens). Surely **CONSEQUENCES** do matter, and arguably there has to be a consequential element to Kant when we imagine universalising an imperative.

Possible Exam Questions

1. "Kantian ethics is not helpful in providing practical guidelines for making moral decisions". Discuss

2. Evaluate to what extent duty can be the sole basis for a moral action.

3. "Kantian ethics is too abstract to be useful in practical ethical decision-making'. Discuss

4. "In neglecting the role of emotions in favour of pure reason, Kantian ethics fails to give a realistic account for our human nature". Discuss

Key Quotes - Kant

1. "It is impossible to conceive of anything in the world good without qualification except the good will". Immanuel Kant

2. "Two things fill me with wonder, the starry hosts above and the moral law within". Immanuel Kant

3. "Kant places the stern voice of duty at the heart of the moral life". Robert Arrington

4. "If our moral sense were based merely on feelings, it would not only vary from person to person – just as some gentlemen prefer blondes and others don't – but could also vary within a person according to his state of health and experiences". Peter Rickman

5. "There remain the categorical imperatives, which derive their authority from reason itself; and the only thing reason abstracted from actual information about specific conditions can command is consistency." Peter Rickman

6. "The highest created good is a world where rational beings are happy and worthy of happiness". Immanuel Kant

7. "To have any goal of action is an act of freedom". Immanuel Kant

8. "With sufficient ingenuity almost every precept can be consistently universalised". Alasdair MacIntyre

9. "There is more to the moral point of view than being willing to universalise one's rules". William Frankena

Confusions - Kant

1. "Duty means blind obedience". This is what Adolf Eichmann implied in his trial in 1962 - but it's not Kant's view of duty which involves reasoning through the **UNIVERSALISABILITY** of your action and treating all human beings with equal respect.

2. "Duty means ignoring emotion". This is a possible reading of Kant, but not the only one. Another reading is to say that Kant saw duty as the primary motive and so long as emotions don't conflict with duty then having moral emotions is fine - just don't base your reason on emotion as it is unreliable.

3. 'Kantian ethics is deontological". William Frankena classified Kant as deontological and it is true Kant argues for unconditional commands (categoricals). But when we universalise we can't help thinking about consequences - there is a consequential dimension to Kant. Whether we have done our duty from the right motive is deontological - but determining the right duty needs a **TELEOLOGICAL** approach.

Bentham's Act Utilitarianism

Key Terms

- **PLEASURE** the one intrinsic good, according to Bentham

- **GREATEST HAPPINESS PRINCIPLE** to act to maximise the greatest happiness of the greatest number - the fundamental principle of utilitarian ethics

- **HEDONIC CALCULUS** a way of quantifying pleasure by seven criteria

- **TELEOLOGICAL** a theory which relates goodness to ends or purposes

- **CONSEQUENTIALIST** identifying goodness by the results of an action

- **EMPIRICAL** a scientific word implying morality can be tested and measured

Background

BENTHAM (1748-1832) was a social reformer who believed that the law should serve human needs and welfare. Where **JUSTICE** was **RETRIBUTIVE** he wanted to see it REFORMING and acting as a **DETERRENCE** – there had to be a real social benefit outweighing the pain to the criminal, and with a better **DISTRIBUTION** of resources, but all in the cause of the **GREATEST HAPPINESS PRINCIPLE (GHP)** –

the motive was to reduce suffering and increase happiness for everyone. The theory is **TELEOLOGICAL** because it measures likely consequences of **ACTIONS**, and **HEDONIC** because Bentham believed pleasure (Greek: hedon) was the key motive and could be quantified. So there is an **EMPIRICAL**, objective measure of goodness.

Motivation

There is one **MORAL** good – pleasure, and one evil – pain. "Nature has placed mankind under two **SOVEREIGN** masters, pain and pleasure". Right actions are on balance pleasurable, wrong actions are on balance painful. Bentham's is therefore a theory of **PSYCHOLOGICAL HEDONISM** (Hedonism - pleasure-seeking).

Hedonic Calculus

The **HEDONIC CALCULUS** is a way of measuring pleasure and pain, so the consequences of an act can be assessed as a score in units of happiness called **HEDONS** (plus for pleasure, minus for pain). The seven criteria are (acronym **PRRICED**): **P**urity, **R**ichness, **R**eliability, **I**ntensity, **C**ertainty, **E**xtent, **D**uration. In this assessment "everyone is to count as one and no-one as more than one" (Bentham), so there is strict **EQUALITY**.

Quantitative Pleasure

Bentham believed "pushpin is as good as poetry" (pushpin – a pub game = playing a slot machine in today's terms). Pleasure is purely **QUANTITATIVE** so we can't award more hedons to listening to Mozart or painting a picture or grasping philosophy. Mill, who was saved from mental breakdown by **WORDSWORTH**'s poetry, really objected to this. According to Bentham, we can compare a small child's delight in a new toy with someone else's delight in a new girlfriend. A **PIG** enjoying a good wallow is of more value than **SOCRATES** having a sightly sad think. Hence "the pig philosophy".

Pleasure Machines

JCC SMART (1973:18-21) asks us to imagine a pleasure machine where we can be wired up every day and passively enjoy every pleasure imaginable (note-addiction often operates like this as a kind of refuge in a supposed pleasure - like drink). **ALDOUS HUXLEY** wrote of a brave new world where people popped **SOMA** tablets to make them happy (there were 41m antidepressant prescriptions last year in the UK). Bentham can have no problems with this, but **MILL** saw happiness as a wider idea involving **ACTIVITY**, and realistic goals and expectations (closer to what my therapist might advise or what **ARISTOTLE** argues).

Strengths - Bentham

There is a **SIMPLICITY** in Bentham's calculation, and a radical **EQUALITY**. The **TELOS** of increasing human welfare is attractive and **COMMON SENSE**. His ideas drove **SOCIAL REFORM** – and he designed a more humane prison called a **PANOPTICON** – never built in the UK, but in Barcelona. There is a lack of snobbery in his classification of all pleasures as **EQUALLY VALID** – why should Mozart be thought better than Rap music (at least in giving pleasure)?

purity
remote-ness
reprod-ucability
intensity
certainty
extent
duration
HEDON-O-METER
JERRY BENTHAM'S
12 FRUIT SLURPER

Weaknesses

Bentham focuses only on **ACTIONS** so we have to keep on calculating (he doesn't allow us to have **RULES** to make life easier). He equates **PLEASURE** with **HAPPINESS** – but they don't seem to be equivalent (ask the athlete training for the Olympics whether the toil is pleasurable – but it doesn't mean a lack of contentment with training). We can always ask "you're going to the nightclub, but is that a **GOOD** idea?" (Good meaning "promoting your welfare"). Bentham implies pleasure is **MEASURABLE** (it isn't - how can we compare my hedon with yours?). Finally, he has no answer for Smart's **PLEASURE MACHINE** or Huxley's **SOMA** tablet (of course, they were writing two centuries later so even if his stuffed skeleton, residing in a cupboard in London University, could talk, we don't know what it would say!).

Key Quotes - Bentham

1. "Nature has placed mankind under two sovereign masters, pain and pleasure. It is for them to point out what we ought to do as well as determine what we should do". Jeremy Bentham, Principles of Morals

2. "In every human breast, self-regarding interest is predominant over social interest; each person's own individual interest over the interests of all other persons taken together". Jeremy Bentham, Book of Fallacies, p 392

3. "The community is a fictitious body," and it is but "the sum of the interests of the several members who compose it". Jeremy Bentham, Principles of Morals

4. "Prejudice apart, the game of pushpin is of equal value with the arts and sciences of music and poetry. If the game of pushpin furnishes more pleasure, it is more valuable than either". Jeremy Bentham, Principles of Morals

Mill's Rule Utilitarianism

Key Terms

- **ACT UTILITARIANISM** (AU) measuring the utility of an individual act

- **RULE UTILITARIANISM** (RU) focusing on the rules which maximise social happiness

- **RIGHTS** legal obligations which maximise social utility

- **JUSTICE** certain principles, practices and rights which according to Mil guarantee social utility

- **QUALITATIVE PLEASURE** pleasure can be evaluated according to its social value as 'higher' (intellectual) and 'lower' (bodily)

Weak Rule Utilitarianism

The weak **RULE UTILITARIANISM** of John Stuart Mill (1806-73) is a **TELEOLOGICA**L (telos = goal) theory based on a definition of goodness as the **BALANCE** of happiness over misery.

This is a measurable, **EMPIRICAL** idea – measure the happiness effects of likely consequences – giving an **OBJECTIVE** measure of goodness.

Mill was against the **INTUITIONISTS** which he found too **SUBJECTIVE**. Mill argues that happiness is most likely to be maximised by generally following a set of **RULES** which society has found, by experience, maximise utility. But the rules can develop and in cases of moral dilemmas, we should revert to being **ACT UTILITARIANS** (so weak **RU**).

Mill & Bentham

Mill disliked three aspects of **BENTHAM**'s version.

1. The swinish implications of categorising all pleasures as of equal value – drinking beer v. listening to Mozart.

2. The emphasis on pleasure alone, as Mill was influenced by **ARISTOTLE**'s views on virtue (eg the importance of **SYMPATHY** for others).

3. The problem of **JUSTICE** and **RIGHTS** – how do we prevent one innocent person or group being sacrificed for the general happiness of the majority? So Mill devotes the last chapter of his essay to **JUSTICE**.

Mill On Happiness

Mill's definition of a happy life has three elements – pleasure (varied and rich) and absence of pain, **AUTONOMY** (the free choice of a life goal), and **ACTIVITY** (motivated by virtues like sympathy eg Mill used to hand out leaflets advising about contraception and campaigned for women's rights).

"**HAPPINESS** is not a life of rapture, but moments of such, in an existence with few and transitory pains, many and various pleasures, with a decided predominance of the **ACTIVE** over the passive, and having as a foundation of the whole, not to expect more from life than it is capable of bestowing". JS Mill, Utilitarianism

Higher And Lower Pleasures

Mill was saved from a nervous breakdown in his 20s by the **ROMANTIC MOVEMENT** eg Wordsworth's Lyrical Ballads. To him poetry was infinitely superior to **PUSHPIN** (a pub game). So "better to be Socrates dissatisfied than a fool satisfied". T

he **LOWER** bodily pleasures (food, sex, drink, football) were of less value than the **HIGHER** pleasures (reading, thinking, listening to Mozart).

So Mill followed **ARISTOTLE** in seeing education as of vital importance (the supreme Greek value is **CONTEMPLATION** to gain wisdom). Only a person who'd experienced both could really judge the difference in **QUALITY** (so we say qualitative pleasure is superior to quantitative). He called those who hadn't experienced both "inferior beings". Does this make Mill a snob?

Rules

Mill has been called an "inconsistent utilitarian" (Alasdair MacIntyre) – because as his essay goes on he moves from **ACT** to **RULE** utilitarianism. We use generations of past experience to form rules, so we don't have to do a calculation to know whether murder or theft is "right". We inherit **BELIEFS** "and the beliefs which have thus come down are the **RULES** of morality for the multitude" (JS Mill). These are not fixed but "admit of continual improvement" – so not **ABSOLUTE**.

The **FIRST PRINCIPLE** is utility (or the Greatest Happiness Principle) and then **SECONDARY PRINCIPLES** (rules) come from this and are constantly evaluated against the first principle. Just as navigation is based on astronomy (Mill's own analogy) doesn't mean the sailor goes back to the stars every time – no he uses an **ALMANAC** – so, argues Mill, human beings follow a code book of rules passed down from previous generations as the best way to be happy.

But if the depth sounder disagrees with the chart datum (rules of past chart-plotter's experience) we revert to being act utilitarians (my analogy).

Justice

Bernard **WILLIAMS** argued that Utilitarianism violates our **MORAL INTEGRITY** by encouraging us to do things we would find repulsive – like his example of Jim who is invited to kill one Indian as an honoured guest in order to save nineteen others. This is the problem of **INJUSTICE** – the Southern States may have enjoyed lynching innocent people in the 1920s but this doesn't make it right.

Mill argues that unhappiness is caused by selfishness, by people "acting only for themselves", and that for a person to be happy they need "to cultivate a fellow feeling with the collective interests of mankind" and "in the **GOLDEN RULE** of Jesus we find the whole ethics of utility" (JS Mill).

So we need to defend personal **RIGHTS** and "Justice is a name for certain moral requirements, which, regarded collectively, stand higher in the scale of **SOCIAL UTILITY**, and are therefore of more paramount obligation, than any others", and " justice is a name for certain classes of **MORAL RULES**, which concern the essentials of human well-being".

Rights, justice and the virtue of sympathy stop selfish self-interest destroying the happiness of others. So we escape the problem of Jim and the Indians.

Act Or Rule?

LOUIS POJMAN argues (2006:111) that we can adopt a **MULTILEVEL** approach (this is what Mill seems to be doing in talking about **PRIMARY** and **SECONDARY** principles). So we can have three levels if we wish: rules of thumb to live by which generally maximise utility, a second set of rules for resolving conflicts between these, and a third process – an **ACT** utilitarian one, for assessing a difficult situation according to the Greatest Happiness Principle (eg lying to save a friend). But in this way philosophers like **J.O.URMSON** argue that **RULE** utilitarianism collapses into **ACT** utilitarianism. Mill might counter that we don't have the time, the wisdom, or the resources to keep calculating every action and this multilevel approach is therefore realistic and practical in a way that **KANT**'s deontology is unrealistic and impractical because it cannot handle **MORAL DILEMMAS**.

Strengths

RATIONALITY and **PRACTICALITY** Utilitarian ethics rests on a rational calculation of numbers of people whose pleasure or happiness is maximised. There is a clarity and simplicity to this.

EQUALITY is central. Bentham wrote "everyone is to count as one, and no-one as more than one". This radical idea implies that everyone has equal weight in the utility calculation.

MILL adds equal **RIGHTS**. Suppose, on an equal vote, you all vote for my dismissal (or even death) in line with maximising general happiness? Mill argues this sort of law would violate rights and such a society would not be one that we'd choose to live in - it would be miserable. "The utilitarian emphasis on impartiality must be a part of any defensible moral theory". (Rachels, 2006:114). Finally, utilitarianism takes account of the **FUTURE** – issues of climate change, potential future wars and famines all suggest we need an ethical theory that takes into account those yet unborn.

Weaknesses

MOTIVE, "why should I maximise pleasure or happiness?" We can't agree how to define pleasure or happiness. Bentham and Mill don't notice the difficulty of the concept of "pleasure" a fatal objection at the outset", Anscombe (1958:2). Then there is a difficulty in making me think of the interests (happiness) of others. Mill tries to bring "sympathy" in as a kind of virtue or psychological motive.

DISTRIBUTION problems emerge when I try to maximise **TOTAL** not **AVERAGE** happiness – eg low tax for the rich may raise the total but reduce average happiness, because the 10% super rich are much, much happier.

Finally **CONSEQUENCES** are hard to calculate if you don't have the omniscience of God. The **IRAQ WAR** may have seemed justifiable by the Greatest Happiness Principle - but looking with hindsight we might argue - better a Saddam Hussein in power than a million deaths?

Possible Exam Questions

1. Evaluate the view that utilitarianism does not provide a helpful way of solving moral dilemmas.

2. "The application of the greatest happiness principle in specific situations is not a sufficient guide to the good action". Discuss

3. "Pleasure is not quantifiable". Discuss

4. To what extent does utilitarian ethics provide a useful guide to issues surrounding business ethics?

Key Quotes - Mill's Utilitarianism

1. "It is better to be a human being dissatisfied than a pig satisfied; better Socrates dissatisfied than a fool satisfied". J.S.Mill, Utilitarianism

2. "Happiness is...moments of rapture...in an existence of few and transitory pains, many and various pleasures, with a predominance of the active over the passive..not to expect more from life than it is capable of bestowing". J.S. Mill, Utilitarianism

3. "Whatever we adopt as the fundamental principle of Morality refers to the first-order beliefs and practices about good and evil by means of which we guide our behaviour. For morality, we require subordinate principles to apply it by". (Fundamental principle = happiness is good, subordinate principles = rules) J.S. Mill, Utilitarianism

4. "By the improvement of education, the feeling of unity with our fellow-creatures shall be as deeply rooted in our character, as the horror of crime is in an ordinarily well brought up young person". (= sympathy) JS Mill, Utilitarianism

5. "To have a right, then, is, I conceive, to have something which society should defend me in possession of. If the objector asks why? I can give no other answer than general utility". J.S.Mill, Utilitarianism

6. "Justice is a name for certain moral requirements, which, regarded collectively, stand higher in the scale of social utility, than any others". J.S.Mill, Utilitarianism

7. "I account the justice which is grounded on utility to be the chief part, and incomparably the most sacred and binding part, of all morality." J.S.Mill, Utilitarianism

8. "Because our relation to the world is partly given by moral feelings, and by a sense of what we can or cannot "live with", to regard those feelings....as happening outside one's moral self is to lose one's moral identity; to lose one's integrity". (Bernard Williams, Utilitarianism For and Against pg 104)

9. "In the golden rule of Jesus of Nazareth we find the whole ethics of utility". JS Mill, Utilitarianism

Confusions - Mill

1. Was Mill an Act or Rule Utilitarian? He is sometimes described as a **WEAK RULE UTILITARIAN**. Mill believed that generally we should follow the rule as this reflects society's view of what maximises happiness from past social experience. But when a pressing utilitarian need arises we should break the rule and so become an act utilitarian.

2. "Mill took Bentham's view that happiness equates to pleasure". Sometimes Mill seems to argue this, but it's truer to say Mill's view is close to **ARISTOTLE**'s that happiness means "personal and social flourishing". So to Mill the individual cannot be happy without the guarantee of certain rules and rights and clear goals to aim for.

3. "Utilitarianism ignores individual rights". Mill would vigorously deny this: rights are essential for the happy society and the happy society generally, with a sense of security, is essential for happy individuals. However, a Benthamite view of individual **ACT UTILITARIANISM** is subject to this criticism (as is US foreign policy which included Guantanamo Bay and Rendition), because many people's pleasure outweighs one or two people's pain (it's the **BALANCE** of pleasure over pain that matters morally).

4. "Utilitarianism is a form of egoism". Utilitarianism escapes this criticism for two reasons: there is an impartiality as "everyone to count as one" and secondly, because the virtue of **SYMPATHY** as a moral feeling is fundamental to my concern for your welfare.

Situation Ethics - Christian Relativism

Situation Ethics is a **NORMATIVE** theory (tells you what is right/wrong – what you ought to do), that is **TELEOLOGICAL** and **CONSEQUENTIALIST** (acts are right or wrong if they bring about good/bad consequences, or can be seen as instrumentally good/bad) and **RELATIVIST** (there are no universal rules as actions depend on circumstances; there is just one general universal value – that of agape love). It is also **CHRISTIAN**, based on the principle of sacrificial love (**AGAPE**).

Introduction

Joseph Fletcher (1966) argued there are three approaches to ethics:

1. **LEGALISTIC** – someone who follows absolute rules and laws. Fletcher rejects this as it leads to **UNTHINKING OBEDIENCE** and needs elaborate systems of exceptions and compromises.

2. **ANTINOMIAN** – (nomos is Greek for law, so anti-law) or someone who rejects all rules and laws (Fletcher rejects this as it would lead to social **CHAOS**).

3. **SITUATIONAL** – Fletcher argues that each individual situation is different and absolute rules are too demanding and restrictive. Instead we should decide what is the most **LOVING** course of

action (**AGAPE**). The Situationist has respect for laws and tradition, but they are only guidelines to how to achieve this loving outcome, and thus they may be broken if the other course of action would result in more love.

However, Situation Ethics is not **FULLY** relativist: it has an absolute principle (love) that is non-negotiable.

Origins Of Agape In The New Testament

William Temple wrote "there is only one ultimate and invariable duty; and its formula is this: "thou shalt love thy neighbour as thyself" (1917:206). He went on: "what acts are right depends on circumstances" (1934:405). Fletcher was inspired by Temple but also argues that love is the fundamental controlling norm. There is a case for arguing this from the New Testament.

- Love is the heart of God's **CHARACTER**. "God is love" (1 John 4:8). This echoes the Old Testament description of God as one "abounding in steadfast love and faithfulness" (Exodus, 34:8) in his revelation to Moses.

- Love is the fulfilling of the **LAW**. Love interprets the commandments and allows us sometimes to break them. In John 8 Jesus refuses to allow them to stone an adulterous woman in direct breach of Leviticus 20:10.

- Love is the heart of a controlling **PARABLE** of the Good Samaritan., (Luke 10). "Controlling" in the sense that Jesus' own sacrificial love mirrors that of the outsider who did all he could to help the victim, as priests and officials passed by, and so the parable 'controls' our interpretation of the entire mission of Christ.

- Love is Jesus' new **COMMAND** (John 13:34) - 'a new commandment I give to you to love one another as I have loved you".

- Sacrificial love (**AGAPE**) is the highest form of love; "Greater love has no man than this, that he lay down his life for his friends". John 15:13

- Love is also the supreme **VIRTUE** in the writings of Paul, with many characteristics (kindness, patience, forgiveness, positivity, hopefulness, perserverance), (1 Corinthians 13).

- Love is given to us by the **SPIRIT** of love, says Paul - the Holy Spirit. (Romans 5:5)

So although the Greeks had several words for love - friendship, family love, erotic love - the greatest moral value is given to **AGAPE**.

Four Working Principles

In Situation Ethics there are **FOUR WORKING PRINCIPLES** (Fletcher's own term).

1. **PRAGMATISM** – (what you propose must be practical – work in practice).

2. **RELATIVISM** – (there are no fixed, absolute rules – all decisions are relative to **AGAPE** love. If love demands that you steal food, then you should steal food. Notice this is special meaning of relativism - Fletcher calls his theory 'principled relativism' because every action is made relative to the one principle of agape love.

3. **POSITIVISM** – (Kant and Natural Law are based on reason as both theories argue reason can uncover the right course of action). Fletcher disagrees with this: you have to start with a **POSITIVE** choice or commitment – you need to want to do good. There is no rational answer to the question "why should I love?" We accept this norm by faith.

4. **PERSONALISM** – (people come first: you cannot sacrifice people to rules or laws)

Six Fundamental Principles

1. Nothing is good in itself except **LOVE** (it is the only thing that is absolutely good, the only thing with intrinsic value).

2. Jesus replaced the law with love or **AGAPE** ("The ruling norm of Christian decision is love, nothing else". Joseph Fletcher).

3. Love and **JUSTICE** are the same thing (if love is put into practice it can only result in fair treatment and fair distribution).

4. Love desires the good of **OTHERS** (it does not have favourites, but this doesn't mean we have to **LIKE** them).

5. Only the **END JUSTIFIES THE MEANS** (if an action causes harm, it is wrong. If good comes of it, it is right).

6. Love's decisions are made in each **SITUATION**.

Conscience

Fletcher argues conscience has many potential meanings:

- **THE VOICE OF GOD** - as in the writings of Cardinal John Henry Newman.

- **PRACTICAL REASON** or phronesis - one of two meanings in the writings of Thomas Aquinas.

- **AN INSTINCT** we are born with. Aquinas' other word for conscience is **SYNDERESIS,** meaning an innate conscience.

- **AS A VERB** - Fletcher rejects the idea of conscience as a 'faculty' and argues it is like a verb reflecting our actions in doing loving things: 'there is no conscience; 'conscience' is merely a word for our attempts to make decisions creatively, constructively, fittingly'. (1966:53)

Strengths Of Situation Ethics

It takes **INDIVIDUALS** and their needs seriously. It's also **FLEXIBLE** and also allows us to make judgements in situations where two moral principles conflict. **LOVE** is an important value somewhat neglected by other theories, as the motive of sympathy in Mill's utilitarian ethics is not quite as strong as the **AGAPE** of Joseph Fletcher.

Weaknesses Of Situation Ethics

LOVE is a very demanding value to place at the centre of your ethics - can anyone love sacrificially all the time? Mustn't we be selfish some of the time? Like all **CONSEQUENTIALIST** theories it's impossible to calculate into the future making this particular love calculation **IMPOSSIBLE**. William Barclay argues that Fletcher fails to realise the value of law - as an expression fo the collective wisdom of generations before us, so the moral law is a guide which we shouldn't throw away so easily. Law also defines the **FABRIC** of society.

Possible Exam Questions

1. "Situation ethics is too demanding as a system of ethical decision-making". Discuss

2. "Goodness is only defined by asking - how is agape best served". Discuss

3. "Agape is not so much a religious idea as an equivalent to saying 'I want the best for you'". Discuss

4. Evaluate the extent to which situation ethics is individualistic and subjective.

Key Quotes - Situation Ethics

1. "Love alone is always good and right in every situation". Joseph Fletcher (Situation Ethics, 1966:69)

2. "Faith, hope and love abide, these three, but the greatest of all is love". 1 Corinthians 13:13

3. "God is love". 1 John 4:8

4. "A new commandment I give to you, that you love one another". John 13:34

5. "Love your neighbour as yourself". Jesus replied, 'Go and do likewise". Luke 10:27,28

6. "There can be and often is a conflict between law and love". Joseph Fletcher (1966:70)

7. "Too much law means the obliteration of the individual; too much individualism means a weakening of the law...there is a place for law as the encourager of morality". William Barclay, Ethics in a Permissive Society p189

8. In 1952 **POPE PIUS XII** called situation ethics "an individualistic and subjective appeal to the concrete circumstances of actions to justify decisions in opposition to the **NATURAL LAW** or God's revealed will'.

9. "High authority has held that a starving man should rather steal a loaf than die of hunger". William Temple (referring to Aquinas)

10. "Every moral act must be good or evil by reason of some circumstance". Thomas Aquinas (de Malo; Q2 A5c)

Some Possible Confusions

1. "Situation ethics is a form of relativism". Fletcher denies this as he argues it is 'principled relativism' - meaning that the supreme norm of love is applied to situations and made relative to need and circumstances. There is thus one absolute norm - **AGAPE.** This is not relativism in the sense of the denial of objective truth, it is relativism in the sense of 'goodness is relative to the situation' (a relativism of application not of norms).

2. "Situation ethics is a religious ethic". It is true that **AGAPE** is a controlling norm of the **NEW TESTAMENT**. Also the parable of the Good Samaritan (Luke 10) appears to be a form of situationism 'go and do likewise', says Jesus, which seems to mean 'go and work out love in the situations you find yourself'. When Fletcher gave up Christianity he still argued that the non-Christian will equate goodness with an idea such as Aristotle's **EUDAIMONIA** (flourishing) whereas the Christian would always maintain **AGAPE** as the supreme norm. So there may be a difference there between atheistic situationism and religious forms.

3. "Jesus was a situationist". It is true that Jesus overthrows some elements of the **LEVITICAL CODE** of law such as stoning adulterers, the uncleanness of certain types of food (such as pork), the uncleanness of certain types of people (such as menstruating women). It is also true that the parable of the **GOOD SAMARITAN** promotes a situationist ethic. However, he also said "I came not to abolish the law but to fulfil the law" (Matthew 5:17). This implies that the fundamental principles of the law such as justice, truth and equality are perfectly fufilled in Jesus, even if he rejects some of the ritualistic practices.

Euthanasia

Definitions

- **EUTHANASIA** (Greek = good death) is the practice of ending life to reduce pain and suffering (so "mercy killing").

- **VOLUNTARY** euthanasia = when a patient's death is caused by another person eg doctor with the **EXPLICIT CONSENT** of the patient. The patient request must be **VOLUNTARY** (acting without coercion, pressure) **ENDURING** (lasts some time or is repeated over time) and **COMPETENT** (they have the mental capacity to choose). A variation on euthanasia is **PHYSICIAN-ASSISTED SUICIDE** – this differs from euthanasia as the doctor will help the patient to commit suicide (eg set up the apparatus), but the final act of killing is done by the patient.

- **NON-VOLUNTARY** euthanasia is done without the patient's consent, because they are not competent or able to give the consent (eg in a coma, on a life support machine). The doctor and/or the family may take the decision. A famous test case was that of **TONY BLAND** who was in a persistent vegetative state following the 1989 Hillsborough football disaster.

- **INVOLUNTARY** euthanasia is performed **AGAINST** the wishes of the patient. This is widely opposed and illegal in the UK.

Active Or Passive

ACTIVE euthanasia is the direct and **DELIBERATE** killing of a patient.

PASSIVE euthanasia is when life-sustaining treatment is withdrawn or withheld.

This distinction may also be described as the difference between an **ACT** and an **OMISSION** (failing to act) and between **KILLING** and **ALLOWING TO DIE**. Some, such as James Rachels, argue there is no real difference – if anything passive euthanasia (withdrawal of treatment) is worse because it leads to a longer, drawn out death and so more suffering potentially. **DAME CICELY SAUNDERS** (who founded the hospice movement) argues that it is unnecessary for anyone to suffer a painful death with modern drugs. A counter-argument is that many doctors already hasten death (eg by doubling a morphine dose): under the doctrine of **DOUBLE EFFECT** (part of Natural Law theory), if the intention is to alleviate pain and a secondary effect to kill someone, the doctor is not guilty of any crime.

Legal Position

Until 1961 suicide was illegal in the UK. The **1961 SUICIDE ACT** legalised suicide but made it illegal to assist.

The **NETHERLANDS** and **SWITZERLAND** allow voluntary euthanasia (active and passive) and physician-assisted suicide. The **DIGNITAS** clinic in Switzerland helped 107 British people to die in 2010. **DR ANNE TURNER** (aged 66) was one such person in 2009 – subject of the docu-drama "A Short Stay in Switzerland". No-one has ever been prosecuted in the UK for helping a relative or friend go to Switzerland.

In 2010 Director of Public Prosecutions **KEIR STARMER** confirmed that relatives of people who kill themselves will not face prosecution as long as they do not maliciously encourage them and assist only a "clear settled and informed wish" to commit suicide. The move came after the Law Lords backed multiple sclerosis sufferer Debbie Purdy's call for a policy statement on whether people who help someone commit suicide should be prosecuted.

Keir Starmer concluded: "There are **NO GUARANTEES** against prosecution and it is my job to ensure that the most vulnerable people are protected while at the same time giving enough information to those people like Mrs Purdy who want to be able to make informed decisions about what actions they may choose to take".

The **OREGON RULES** are another attempt to legalise assisted suicide by laying down conditions under which it will be allowed in US law.

Sanctity Of Life: Bible

The Bible argues that life is a gift from God. Humans are created in the **IMAGE OF GOD** (Genesis 1:27) and the **INCARNATION** (God taking human form – John 1:14) shows the sacred value of human life. Human life is a **GIFT** or **LOAN** from God (Job 1:21 "The Lord gave and the Lord has taken away"). We should also show **RESPECT** for human life: "thou shalt not murder" (Exodus 20:13). We should also "choose life" (Deuteronomy 30). Finally, Christian love (**AGAPE**) is crucial (1 Corinthians 13 "the greatest value of all is love"). We should protect human life (the parable of the Good Samaritan) particularly as God gave his only son to redeem us (bring us back from sin and death) and give us the gift of "life in all its fullness".

Sanctity Of Life

- The **NATURAL LAW** view argues that there is a **PRIMARY PRECEPT** to "preserve life" and views life as an **INTRINSIC** good. Euthanasia is therefore wrong and the Catholic Church forbids both active and passive euthanasia as "contrary to the dignity of the human person and the respect due to God, his creator" (Catechism of the Roman Catholic Church). However, the **DOCTRINE OF DOUBLE EFFECT** might accept the shortening of human life (eg if the intention is to relieve pain, secondary effect to kill) so long as it is only a **FORESEEN BUT UNINTENDED RESULT**. The Catholic Church also makes a distinction between **ORDINARY MEANS** (ordinary, usual medical treatments) and **EXTRAORDINARY MEANS** (treatments that are dangerous, a huge burden, or disproportionate). It is morally acceptable to stop extraordinary means, as "it is the refusal of over-zealous treatment".

- **ROMAN CATHOLIC** version of Natural law: "Discontinuing medical procedures that are burdensome, dangerous, extraordinary, or disproportionate to the expected outcome can be legitimate; it is the refusal of "over-zealous" treatment. Here one does not will to cause death; one's inability to impede it is merely accepted. The decisions should be made by the patient if he is competent and able or, if not, by those legally entitled to act for the patient, whose reasonable will and legitimate interests must always be respected." Catholic Catechism 2278

- **HUMANIST ARGUMENTS** Following Mill's rule utilitarianism, we could argue that a. A general rule should be in place for social happiness prohibiting euthanasia (so the elderly don't feel under pressure or depressed people feel the temptation). But, b. In specific cases near the end of life doctor's using their discretion should hasten death. This is the present UK situation, which can be justified by rule utilitarian (non-Christian) arguments, giving a modified humanist sanctity of life view.

Quality Of Life: Situation Ethics

JAMES RACHELS argues that the sanctity of life tradition places too much value on human life and there are times (eg with abortion and euthanasia) when this is unhelpful. He makes a distinction between **BIOLOGICAL LIFE** ("being alive" = functioning biological organism) and **BIOGRAPHICAL LIFE** ("having a life" = everything that makes us who we are). He says that what matters is biographical life and if this is already over (for example in a **PERSISTENT VEGETATIVE STATE = PVS**), then taking away biological life is acceptable.

PETER SINGER, a preference utilitarian, argues that the worth of human life varies (the value of human life is not a sacred gift but depends on its **QUALITY**). A low quality of life (judged by the patient) can justify them taking their life or justify someone else doing it for them.

SITUATION ETHICS would also take quality of life as more important than sanctity of life. **PERSONALISM** requires we take a case by case approach, and if someone is suffering in extreme discomfort, then **AGAPE** would dictate that we support their euthanasia. There may however be situations where someone is depressed, for example, where the most loving thing is to persuade them of a life worth living. **PRAGMATISM** demands a case by case and flexible approach. Joseph Fletcher was a himself a pioneer in bioethics and argued: "To bring this matter into the open practice of medicine would harmonise the civil law with medical morals, which must be concerned with the quality of life, not merely its quantity."

Autonomy

JOHN STUART MILL (On Liberty, 1859) argues that individuals should have full **AUTONOMY** (the freedom to make decisions without coercion) so long as it does not harm other people. Individuals cannot be compelled to do things for their own good – "over his own mind-body the individual is sovereign". Those who support voluntary euthanasia believe that personal autonomy and self-determination (choosing what happens to you) are crucial. Any competent adult should be able to decide on the time and manner of their death.

KANT assumes autonomy as one of his three key postulates (together with God and immortality). We are self-legislating, free moral beings. However, he argued in an essay on suicide that suicide was self-contradictory as, if it was universalised, the human race would die out.

DIANE PRETTY argued in a court case in 2002 that Article 1 of the Human Rights Convention (the right to life) included the right to take one's own life. This autonomy argument was rejected by the court. She was paralysed by motor-neurone disease and requested permission for her husband to assist her to die.

Arguments Against Euthanasia

PALLIATIVE CARE – Dame Cicely Saunders argues that there is a better alternative for euthanasia in providing a pain-free death for terminally ill patients. The **HOSPICE** movement may be seen as an alternative, BUT this level of care is not available to everyone, is expensive and cannot fully relieve a patient's suffering (eg for someone who cannot breathe unassisted).

VOLUNTARY AND COMPETENT – some raise questions about voluntary euthanasia. Can the patient ever be free from coercion (eg relatives who want an inheritance or doctors who need to free up resources)? Is the patient likely to be competent (eg when under high doses of medication, or when depressed, or senile). Response would be that there are at least some clear cases when patients **ARE** clearly voluntary (not coerced) and competent. Guidelines such as Starmer's or the **OREGON RULES** require a certain time period of repeated requests to different people, which are then independently confirmed.

SLIPPERY SLOPE – this is the argument that once allowed, the outcome will be a process of a further decline in respect for human life and will end with the practice of non-voluntary euthanasia for the elderly seen as "unaffordable" by the working majority. A response might be that there is a clear difference between voluntary and non-voluntary euthanasia. Is there any evidence of a slippery slope in the US state of Oregon or Switzerland? The rules on assisted suicide are drawn up precisely to stop the slide into widespread disrespect for human life. Note this is an **EMPIRICAL, CONSEQUENTIALIST** argument about probabilities.

DOCTOR-PATIENT RELATIONSHIP – some argue that doctors have a duty to preserve life (the **HIPPOCRATIC OATH**). Euthanasia will undermine the trust between patient and doctor if there is a fear that they will seek to end their life. However, as with abortion, there will remain doctors opposed to euthanasia which a patient could always choose, and it is highly unlikely that GPs will have any say in the process of mercy killing.

Some Possible Questions

1. Natural Law is superior to situation ethics in its treatment of issues surrounding euthanasia". Discuss

2. "Autonomy as an ideal is unrealistic. No-one is perfectly autonomous". Discuss with reference to the ethical issue of euthanasia.

3. "Sanctity of human life is the core principle of medical ethics". Discuss

4. "There is no moral difference between actively ending a life by euthanasia and omitting to treat the patient". Discuss

Key Quotes

1. "Euthanasia is contrary to the dignity of the human person and the respect due to God, His creator". Roman Catholic Catechism

2. "The Lord gave, and the Lord takes away; blessed be the name of the Lord". Job 1:21

3. "God created man in His own image". Genesis 1:27

4. "God knit you together in your mother's womb". Psalm 139:6

5. "Discontinuing medical procedures that are burdensome, dangerous, or disproportionate to the expected outcome can be legitimate". Catholic Catechism

6. "Compare a severely defective human infant with a nonhuman animal, we will often find the non-human to have superior capacities". Peter Singer

7. "We see a life of permanent coma as in no way preferable to death". Jonathan Glover

8. "The ability to make complex judgements about benefit requires compassion, experience and an appreciation of the patient's viewpoint". British Medical Association

9. "Once the boundary is crossed it is hard to see how social and commercial pressures do not define the 'volunteers'." Alastair Campbell in Gill, R. ed Euthanasia and the Churches (Cassell, 1998 p 94)

10. 'For all too many people there are good and reasonable grounds for the deepest despair. Where suffering is reasonably perceived to be unbearable, suicide can be morally right". James Gustafson Ethics from a Theocentric Perspective, (Chicago, 1984 p 214)

Business Ethics

Introduction

BUSINESS ETHICS is the critical examination of how people and institutions should behave in the world of commerce e.g. appropriate limits on self-interest, or (for firms) profits, when the actions of individuals or firms affect others. We may examine **CODES** which companies publish, or **BEHAVIOUR** of individuals – but also **CORPORATE CULTURE** (which may contradict the code) and responsibilities to the **ENVIRONMENT** and the developing world created by **GLOBALISATION** of markets and free trade between countries. We are asked to apply the Kantian idea of **UNIVERSALISED** duties and categoricals to business ethics, and utilitarian ideas of calculating net happiness or pleasure. according to **CONSEQUENCES**.

Key Terms

- **PROFIT MOTIVE** - the reward for risk-taking in maximising returns on any investment.

- **STAKEHOLDERS** - any parties affected by a business practice.

- **EXTERNALITIES** - costs or benefits external to the company – pollution is a negative externality.

- **GLOBALISATION** - the interconnection of economies ,

information and culture.

- **MULTINATIONALS** - companies trading in many countries.

Issues

Does the **PROFIT MOTIVE** conflict with ethical practice? Or does good ethics result in good business.

Should the regulation of business be left to **GOVERNMENTS**?

Ben and Jerry's has this **SOCIAL RESPONSIBILITY** statement at its heart: "to operate the company in a way that recognises the role business plays in the wider society and to find innovative ways to improve the life of the wider community". How widely is this view shared?

What happens when **STAKEHOLDER** interests conflict (eg sacking workers to raise shareholder returns?).

In a **GLOBALISED** world should we treat all workers the same irrespective of differences in national laws (think of safety regulations overseas)? Do **MULTINATIONALS** have too much power?

Stake-Holders

A **STAKEHOLDER** is any individual or group who has a stake in the success or failure of a company. It includes **INTERNAL STAKEHOLDERS** (managers, employees) and **EXTERNAL** (the local community, customers, shareholders, suppliers, local authorities,

Government, other countries). For example, the existence of a Tesco store may mean local shopkeepers do better (if more people visit the town) or worse (if business is taken away).

Stakeholder theory suggest we should consider the interests of all stakeholders in the consequences of a decision.

Codes

Most companies have **CODES OF ETHICS** which lay out the rights of different groups and the responsibilities and values of the company. **ETHICAL INVESTORS** only invest in companies that fulfil certain criteria eg **ENVIRONMENTAL** responsibility, and **FAIR TRADE** for overseas workers.

ETHICAL CONSUMERS look for sustainable sources or organic produce. The April 2011 riots in **BRISTOL** against the Tesco local store show how different interests may clash – stakeholders such as local businesses/some customers v. large corporations/ other customers and employees. Does Tesco have an **ETHICAL DUTY** not to destroy local businesses, or a duty to its potential **EMPLOYEES** (jobs) and **CUSTOMERS** (lower prices)? Is there and **ABSOLUTE** principle we can find to judge between them?

Most companies have ethics codes. But do they embody them as virtues?

Cost/Benefit

COST/BENEFIT analysis is a business equivalent to **UTILITARIAN**

ethics, as it seeks to weigh the benefits in money terms of a business decision against the cost. It suffers the same problem: the denial of **INDIVIDUAL RIGHTS** as a moral **ABSOLUTE**.

In the case of **FORD PINTO** (1970s) the cost of a **HUMAN LIFE** was weighed against the number of likely accidents and the cost of a **PRODUCT RECALL**. At $13 a car it was not worth the recall, they decided. But – they didn't calculate **CONSEQUENCES** correctly and valued **HUMAN LIFE** too cheaply – so ended up paying millions in compensation and having to **RECALL** the car anyway.

Unfortunately value has to be placed on a human life in traffic safety, **NHS** budgets etc – it's not economic to place a crash barrier alongside roads adjacent to remote reservoirs – so tragic accidents do occur (e.g in April 2011 four die in a car plunging into a reservoir in Wales).

If environmental costs are too high, will companies pay them or relocate their business?

Externalities

EXTERNALITIES are costs paid (eg pollution) or benefits enjoyed (eg flowers in a roundabout) by someone external to the firm.

Traditionally Governments have taxed and regulated firms to make them comply with their ethical duties: **THE TEN HOURS ACT** (1847 restricts child labour to 10 hrs a day), the **CLEAN AIR ACT** (1956 restricts carbon emissions), the **HEALTH AND SAFETY ACT** (1974 – improved safety standards and penalised non-compliance), the **SEX DISCRIMINATION ACT** (1975 – Equal Pay and opportunity for women).

MILTON FRIEDMAN (economist) argues that companies have a duty only to their shareholders (ie profits) – it is for society to set the other ethical rules. But examples such as **ENRON**, the US energy company that went bankrupt in 2003 after massive fraud, indicate that laws are never enough – individuals need to take **RESPONSIBILITY**.

As environmental regulation increases the cost to companies rises. Yet the USA has still not signed up to immediate carbon emission reduction despite the 1996 **KYOTO** protocol and the **COPENHAGEN** (2008)and **DURBAN** (2011) summits. Although China, Russia and America signed the Durban agreement, this only committed countries to define a future treaty by 2015, which will be binding in 2020.Once again immediate action has been postponed. US Senator Jim Inhofe, who has called climate change "the greatest hoax every perpetrated on the American people", applauded the "complete collapse of the global warming movement and the Kyoto protocol".

Rights

ABSOLUTISTS (eg Kantians) argue for universal human rights that apply everywhere for all time – including workers and communities in third world countries.

Because **GLOBALISATION** includes the free flow of **CAPITAL** to least cost countries, this can include those with corrupt governments or lax health and safety laws. Union Carbide (US firm) plant in **BHOPAL** (1986, India) and **TRAFIGURA** oil waste disposal (2008, Ivory Coast, hydrogen sulphide) illustrate how thousands can die (Bhopal – mustard gas) or go sick (Trafigura) when companies pursue least cost choices to boost **PROFIT**.

Worker and community rights often seem to take second place to **SHAREHOLDER** interests.

Individuals

Individual workers may become **WHISTLEBLOWERS** and expose fraud, corruption, lax standards etc. The RBS sacked their finance director who "didn't fit in" = opposed their lending policy before the **GLOBAL FINANCIAL CRISIS**.

UK banks were 24 hours from collapse in 2008 before a Government rescue plan, in taking on their bad debts. The rescue of **ROYAL BANK OF SCOTLAND** cost £43bn. But in the **EUROZONE** crisis countries act like individuals, with David Cameron vetoing a recent treaty change because of Britain's **NATIONAL INTEREST**. Is there such an idea as **COLLECTIVE** (European) interest?

Individual **CONSCIENCE** may serve the **public good,** but at the cost of their own **SELF-INTEREST** (they're fired). Kantian ethics may help us cling to **ABSOLUTES**, but Utilitarian ethics tends to make us pragmatists as at the **NORMATIVE** level we lie or stay silent to serve a **COLLECTIVE** interest (and we may not have enough sympathy with outsiders to care).

However **ENRON**'s collapse in 2003 brought down auditor **ARTHUR ANDERSEN** as it was implicated in the financial fraud which covered up huge debts, and affected shareholders, employees and pensioners. Sometimes **SHORT -TERMISM** in the utilitarian calculation can have terrible long-term consequences, and the courage of **ERIN BROKOVITCH** in exposing the toxic leaks of **PACIFIC GAS** in an

American town shows how a Kantian sense of duty may have much to teach us in Business affairs, even though it can be risky for an individual to take on powerful corporations. There was one Enron whistleblower - Vice-President Sherron Watkins - but she only blew as far as Chairman Ken Lay.

Future Generations

One of the puzzles of ethics is how we account for the interests of future generations and animals, plants, etc. Both **KANTIAN** and **UTILITARIAN** ethics are traditionally weak on environmental issues (Kant stresses rational autonomous beings as having moral worth, not animals, and utilitarianism sees the environment as having only **INSTRUMENTAL** goodness as a means to human happiness. This may suffer from the problem of **SHORT-TERMISM)**.

UTILITARIANISM however can arguably do better because the long term happiness of the human race is clearly one factor to consider – but how do we know how many people to add in to the calculation? How do we assess the environmental effect of the plastic bag "island" the size of Texas which exists in the central vortex of the **PACIFIC** ocean currents? **SUSTAINABLE DEVELOPMENT** is a new idea – and **CHRISTIAN ETHICS** has arguably suffered from an emphasis on **DOMINION** (Genesis 1:26) = exploit, rather than **STEWARDSHIP** = care for the environment.

Can we provide incentives to this generation to protect future rights of the unborn?

Globalisation

Globalisation is the **INTERCONNECTION** of markets, technology and information across the world. There are said to be five global brands: Nike, Coca-Cola, McDonalds, Levis. However globalisation brings the risk that large companies dominate the political agenda working in their own interest, and also force wages down for third world suppliers. For example, multinationals fund **PRESIDENTIAL** campaigns and the oil industry lobbies ceaselessly to stop any rise in **OIL PRICES** and even, it has been alleged, the development of alternative energy sources.

The economist Amartya Sen has argued that the central issue is "the **UNEQUAL SHARING** in the benefits of globalisation" – that the poor receive an unequal gain from any wealth created. Put another way, less developed countries are exploited for cheap labour in the global market place (compare **WAGES PER HOUR** in China and the UK for example).

Finally there is the question of **REGULATION**. Do multinationals export lax safety standards and poor environmental disciplines to the third world? The examples of **BHOPAL** (1984) and **TRAFIGURA*** (2007) are not encouraging. And could any government have stopped a deregulated world banking system bringing the world economy to the brink of collapse in the crisis of 2008? Short-term profit and excessive **RISK-TAKING** in property lending led to the accumulation of huge debts so that Royal Bank of Scotland was only saved from bankruptcy by a £43bn cash injection by the UK Government.

Are multinationals beyond state regulation? Do they have too much power? What incentive do they have to be ethical?

* In 2007 Trafigura established a foundation to promote environmental concern, rural development programmes and health programmes in the counties where it operated. So far $ 14.5 m dollars has been donated to 36 projects. It is now seeking to create "a lasting, sustainable model for corporate philanthropy", perhaps trying to counteract the bad publicity generated by the waste dumping scandal.

Possible Exam Questions

1. "Kantian ethic of duty is superior to the utilitarian ethic of happiness in dealing with difficult business decisions". Discuss

2. "Corporate social responsibility is ethical window-dressing to cover their greed". Discuss

3. Evaluate the view that capitalism will always exploit human beings in the pursuit of profit.

4. "Globalisation widens the exploitation of human beings by reducing the need for ethically valid regulation of business behaviour". Discuss

Key Quotes

1. 'Corporate executives do not have responsibilities in their business activities, other than to make as much money as possible for their shareholders" Milton Friedman

2. "Good employees are good people". Robert Solomon

3. "The following duties bind the employer: not to look upon their work people as their slaves, but to respect in every man his dignity as a person ennobled by Christian character". Rerum Novarum 1891 (p 20)

4. "It matters that the prevailing ethos of a company brings together corporate purpose and personal values". Cardinal Vincent Nichols

5. 'Serving the public and taking care of own's own employees are not an afterthought of business, but rather its very essence". Robert Solomon

6. 'It is hard to separate businesses being ethical for its own sake with the fact that being ethical might be good for business". Wilcockson and Wilkinson OCR Religious Studies (Hodder, 2016)

7. 'The solidarity that binds all men together as members of a common family make it impossible for wealthy nations to look with indifference upon the hunger, misery and poverty of other nations". Pope John XXIII.

8. "The natural environment is a collective good and the responsibility of everyone". Pope Francis

9. "Man should not consider his material possessions as his own, but as common to all, so as to share them without hesitation when others are in need." Thomas Aquinas (ST II-II, Q46, A2)

10. "The rights and duties of the employers, as compared with the rights and duties of the employed, ought to be the subject of careful consideration." Rerum Novarum 1891 (p 58)

The Four Questions Answered

In the first section of this book I mentioned that there are four questions we need to ask of any moral theory. They spell the acronym **DARM** (**D**erivation, **A**pplication, **R**ealism, **M**otivation).

1. How Is The Idea Of Goodness Derived?

Goodness has to come from somewhere – it is, after all a human construct. The normal candidates are three:

1. God or faith

2. Reason (a priori)

3. Observation or experience (a posteriori, from experience).

RELATIVISTS argue that our idea of goodness comes directly from **CULTURE** (what JL Mackie in Inventing Right and Wrong calls "forms of life") or from **EXPERIENCE** (the utilitarian or situationist view that we judge right and wrong according to circumstances and likely consequences).

NATURAL LAW theorists like **AQUINAS** argue that goodness is partly an **A PRIORI** idea given by God – what he calls synderesis "the intuitive knowledge of first principles", and partly an **A POSTERIORI** idea worked out by experience. We develop our conscience and practical wisdom by looking at circumstances . Natural Law goods are in the end

OBSERVABLE GOODS. We apply the **PRIMARY PRECEPTS** (acronym **POWER**) to situations.

KANT argues that morality is an **A PRIORI** category of the mind like number or cause and effect. Just as we need a concept of **NUMBER** before we can count, so we need a concept of the **CATEGORICAL IMPERATIVE** before we can apply it to the world and synthetic experience where we discover how it works. Morality is therefore **A PRIORI SYNTHETIC**.

UTLITARIANS see goodness as a **TELEOLOGICAL** idea depending on the end we pursue, either **PLEASURE** (the psychological "sovereign two masters, pleasure and pain" of Bentham) or **HAPPINESS** (it is good because most people desire it as an end in itself, says **MILL**). So goodness is measurable, an **OBJECTIVE**, **EMPIRICAL IDEA**, either by counting **HEDONS** (Bentham) or **DESIRES** (Mill). This is therefore a theory appealing to **A POSTERIORI** knowledge because we cannot know consequences without some experience of them.

Notice that only one theory is purely **DEONTOLOGICAL**, Kantian ethics. **NATURAL LAW** has deontological outcomes (the **SECONDARY PRECEPTS**) which come from a **TELEOLOGICAL WORLDVIEW** because in Natural law everything has a proper rational purpose (**TELOS**).

SITUATION ETHICS argues that goodness is accepted by faith as the supreme noram (**POSITIVISM**). Fletcher makes it clear that no intrinsic good can be proved (be it the good will, happiness or anything else). It has to be **POSITED**.

2. How Are The Theories Applied?

RELATIVISTS see goodness as relative to culture or experience and so any situation needs to be applied to the relevant cultural value. These may still be very **REASONABLE** but, argues the relativist, even **REASON** is culturally conditioned and not **PURE** as Kant implied.

NATURAL LAW THEORY applies the five primary precepts (acronym **POWER**) to produce the secondary precepts. So the **P** of **POWER** (preservation of life) yields the **SECONDARY PRECEPT** do not abort, do not commit suicide, do not murder. These are not **ABSOLUTE RULES** as we allow killing in time of war. Ultimately the primary precepts are derived from an idea of **HUMAN FLOURISHING** – what it means for a human being to live well or excellently.

KANT sees right and wrong as something irrational, a **CONTRADICTION** or logical inconsistency. There are two types of self contradiction: the **CONTRADICTION IN NATURE** includes suicide and breaking your promises. These cannot be willed universally without contradiction because **EUTHANASIA** if universalised leads to mass suicide of those in pain, and breaking your promise if universalised leads to the elimination of the idea of promising altogether. A **CONTRADICTION IN WILL** is not illogical, but cannot be universally willed or desired. We could never desire not to help our neighbour in distress because we would always want to be helped when we are in distress.

UTILITARIANS see the right action as one that maximises happiness or pleasure. So we need to examine the likely consequences, count how many are affected by our choice, and then apply the Greatest Happiness Principle. We apply utilitarian principles **CONSEQUENTIALLY**.

SITUATION ETHICS argues for a case by case, pragmatic approach that lies somewhere between **ANTINOMIANISM** (no rules) and **LEGALISM** (strict rules). This is a form of Christian relativism espoused by liberal Christians who see the primary command is to love unconditionally (not to judge or make legal demands). Here the person - their needs and desires - is the key. **PERSONALISM** requires we put them first. This can be described as a from of relativism, as Fletcher himself does - he calls it **PRINCIPLED RELATIVISM** because of the one principle or norm - **AGAPE** love, which is absolute and unchanging. But notice there are other definitions of relativism than Fletcher's - who sees goodness as relative to love and to the consequences and situation.

3. Realism

How realistic are these theories from the perspective of modern sciences such as **PSYCHOLOGY** and **BIOLOGY**?

RELATIVISM fits well the postmodern world where there is no one overarching narrative accepted as true. It also fits **FREUDIAN** psychology where conscience comes from our upbringing and the sense of shame engendered by our parents and teachers. In the postmodern age we are taught to tolerate difference.

NATURAL LAW is often condemned as outdated. However the idea of a shared rational nature is something evolutionary biologists accept. **RICHARD DAWKINS** (The Selfish Gene) talks of a "lust to be nice" coming from our evolved sense of obligation to one another. Is this so different from **AQUINAS'** synderesis rule that we by nature "do good and avoid evil"? Dawkins rejects the **TELEOLOGICAL** nature of Natural Law, as there is no purpose to **EVOLUTION**, he argues, just an endless struggle to survive. But we have inherited an **ALTRUISTIC GENE** from this battle of the genes giving us a shared moral nature. The selfish gene is the self-promoting gene, but for humans, it is in our interest to be moral and so, argues Dawkins, the selfish gene gives us our moral sense and desire to help others.

KANT's ethical theory can be criticised for being **DUALISTIC**. So he sees the world of experience, the **PHENOMENAL** world as opposed to the world of ideas, the **NOUMENAL** world. He also contrasts **REASON** and **EMOTION** in a way that seems to deny moral worth to an action done out of compassion rather than duty alone. The outcome of his theory, that categorical rules are **ABSOLUTE** can also be criticised as unrealistic. In practice we do lie to save someone's life – the goodness is situational, not absolute as Kant suggests.

SITUATION ETHICS suffers from the same two problems as utilitarianism. First, it requires an **IMPARTIALITY** which few are capable of, except Jesus himself. We all ten to rank pople accorsing tot heir closeness to us (family, friends, acquaintances, neighbours and finally strangers). But agape allows no such ranking, otherwise it becomes conditional love. Secondly, it is hard to predict **CONSEQUENCES** and this requires a lifetime of wisdom which few of us possess. William **BARCLAY** (Ethics in a Permissive Society) also points out that social rules embody such wisdom - and those that don't (such as 'homosexuality is wrong') become revised and rejected. But to focus just on individual need and choice is to ignore the important function of rules as guides for us. Ultimately, then Situation ethics may be too demanding and so unrealistic.

4. Motivation: Why Be Moral?

So we come to the final, and perhaps most pressing question. Why be moral at all? Why not live a life of selfish egoism and be a parasite on the goodness of everyone else?

RELATIVISM is a wide and amibiguous concept. Joseph Fletcher (Situation Ethics) defined himself as a relativist (Situation Ethics is a form of Christian relativism). He argued that we are moral out of love for fellow human beings. But this begs the question why I should bother about fellow human beings when it's not in my interest to do so? Fletcher's answer was that we need to convert to the way of love - commitment comes before action. He calls this **THEOLOGICAL POSITIVISM**. Situation ethics is something of a special case and is arguably not a pure form of relativism as it has one **ABSOLUTE** at its centre - agape love.

NATURAL LAW theorists argue from a **TELEOLOGICAL** standpoint. Be moral, they say, because it is reasonable to want to flourish as a human being – to be the most excellent person you can be. A knife should cut well, says Aristotle, and a human being should be rational in order to flourish well. **AQUINAS** argues that our greatest happiness will be found by aligning the natural law with God's eternal law. This will cause us to be a full, complete human being.

KANT takes the stern, dutiful line of obedience to the moral law or **CATEGORICAL IMPERATIVE**. He argues that rational people will freely choose this way as the most logically consistent way of arriving at the **SUMMUM BONUM**, the greatest good. Autonomous human beings will realise that to obey the categorical imperative out of duty is the best way of building the best of all conceivable moral worlds. Like Kant himself, this moral law within should fill us with awe. It's wonderful. The summum bonum is a mixture of virtue (dutifulness) and happiness ultimately only discovered in heaven (Kant's postulate of **IMMORTALITY**).

UTILITARIANS are not agreed on what motivates us. **BENTHAM** thought we were psychological **HEDONISTS** motivated by the prospect of pleasure and avoiding pain. **MILL** disagreed. He thought pleasure and happiness were not the same, as happiness needed clear goals and strenuous activities. Happiness is to be found in challenges met and difficulties overcome – which sometimes can involve discipline and sacrifice. Why bother with the happiness of others? Mill answered, out of **SYMPATHY** for my fellow human beings. "In the Golden Rule of Jesus of Nazareth ("do to others as you would have them do to you" Matthew 7:18)", wrote Mill, "is all the ethics of utility".

SITUATION ETHICS requires us to commit to the motive of unconditional love - we accept this by faith (**POSITIVISM**). Fletcher doesn't talk much about motive, but the Bible suggests 'we love because God first loved us' (1 John 4:19). So we are motivated by what God in Jesus Christ has first done for us in sacrificing his life for us and suffering pain and humiliation on the cross. Moreover Christ's death liberated us from the slavery to sin and set a new agenda for us - to establish the kingdom of God. This is a kingdom of love. And God gave us the Holy Spirit - the spirit of love in our hearts - to empower us when we find it impossible.

Postscript

Andrew Capone is a Director of Religious Studies at St. Simone Stock Catholic School in Maidstone. He has a degree in Philosophy & Religious Studies from the University of Kent and a Masters degree in Classics. He teaches on the Peped revision courses with Peter Baron.

Daniella Dunsmore has a degree in Theology from Christ's College Cambridge.She trained with Teach First, teaching Religious Studies at Sion-Manning Roman Catholic Girls School. She is currently Subject Leader for Religious Studies at Thetford Grammar School.

Peter Baron read Politics, Philosophy and Economics at New College, Oxford and afterwards obtained an MLitt for a research degree in Hermeneutics at Newcastle University. He qualified as an Economics teacher in 1982, and taught ethics at Wells Cathedral School in Somerset from 2006-2012. He is currently a freelance writer and speaker.

In 2007 he set up a philosophy and ethics community dedicated to enlarging the teaching of philosophy in schools by applying the theory of multiple intelligences to the analysis of philosophical and ethical problems. So far over 700 schools have joined the community and over 30,000 individuals use his website every month.

To join the community please join our mailing list on peped.org or follow Peped on Facebook. We welcome contributions and suggestions so that our community continues to flourish and expand.

www.peped.org

Printed in Great Britain
by Amazon